Dorothy McAlpin.
" Dobbs "
1903 .

PONKAPOG
PAPERS

PONKAPOG PAPERS

BY

THOMAS
BAILEY
ALDRICH

TOUT BIEN
OU RIEN

The Riverside
Press

BOSTON
AND NEW YORK
HOUGHTON, MIFFLIN & CO.
MDCCCCIII

TO
FRANCIS BARTLETT

❖

THESE miscellaneous notes and essays are called *Ponkapog Papers* not simply because they chanced, for the most part, to be written within the limits of the old Indian Reservation, but, rather, because there is something typical of their unpretentiousness in the modesty with which Ponkapog assumes to being even a village. The little Massachusetts settlement, nestled under the wing of the Blue Hills, has no illusions concerning itself, never mistakes the cackle of the bourg for the sound that echoes round the world, and no more thinks of rivalling great centres of human activity than these slight papers dream of inviting comparison between themselves and important pieces of literature. Therefore there seems something especially appropriate in the geographical title selected, and if the author's choice of name need further excuse, it is to be found in the alluring alliteration lying ready at his hand.

REDMAN FARM, *Ponkapog*,
  1903.

CONTENTS

CONTENTS

LEAVES
FROM
A NOTE BOOK

LEAVES FROM A NOTE BOOK

IN his Memoirs, Kropótkin states the singular fact that the natives of the Malayan Archipelago have an idea that something is extracted from them when their likenesses are taken by photography. Here is the motive for a fantastic short story, in which the hero — an author in vogue or a popular actor — might be depicted as having all his good qualities gradually photographed out of him. This could well be the result of too prolonged indulgence in the effort to " look natural." First the man loses his charming simplicity; then he begins to pose in intellectual attitudes, with finger on brow; then he becomes morbidly self-conscious, and finally ends in an asylum for incurable egotists. His death might be brought about by a cold caught in going out bareheaded, there being, for the moment, no hat in the market of sufficient circumference to meet his enlarged requirement.

THE evening we dropped anchor in the Bay of Yedo the moon was hanging directly over Yokohama. It was a mother-of-pearl moon, and might have been manufactured by any of the delicate artisans in the Hanchodori quarter. It impressed one as being a very good imitation, but nothing more. Nammikawa, the cloisonné-worker at Tokio, could have made a better moon.

I NOTICE the announcement of a new edition of " The Two First Centuries of Florentine Literature," by Professor Pasquale Villari. I am not acquainted with the work in question, but I trust that Professor Villari makes it plain to the reader how both centuries happened to be first.

4

THE walking delegates of a higher civilization, who have nothing to divide, look upon the notion of property as a purely artificial creation of human society. According to these advanced philosophers, the time will come when no man shall be allowed to call anything his. The beneficent law which takes away an author's rights in his own books just at the period when old age is creeping upon him seems to me a handsome stride toward the longed-for millennium.

SAVE us from our friends — our enemies we can guard against. The well-meaning rector of the little parish of Woodgates, England, and several of Robert Browning's local admirers have recently busied themselves in erecting a tablet to the memory of " the first known forefather of the poet." This lately turned up ancestor, who does not date very far back, was also named Robert Browning, and is described on the mural marble as " formerly footman and

butler to Sir John Bankes of Corfe Castle."
Now, Robert Browning the poet had as good
right as Abou Ben Adhem himself to ask to be
placed on the list of those who love their fellow
men; but if the poet could have been consulted
in the matter he probably would have preferred
not to have that particular footman exhumed.
However, it is an ill wind that blows nobody
good. Sir John Bankes would scarcely have
been heard of in our young century if it had
not been for his footman. As Robert stood day
by day, sleek and solemn, behind his master's
chair in Corfe Castle, how little it entered into
the head of Sir John that his highly respectable
name would be served up to posterity — like a
cold relish — by his own butler! By Robert!

IN the east-side slums of New York, somewhere in the picturesque Bowery district,
stretches a malodorous little street wholly
given over to long-bearded, bird-beaked merchants of ready-made and second-hand clothing.

6

The contents of the dingy shops seem to have revolted, and rushed pell-mell out of doors, and taken possession of the sidewalk. One could fancy that the rebellion had been quelled at this point, and that those ghastly rows of complete suits strung up on either side of the doorways were the bodies of the seditious ringleaders. But as you approach these limp figures, each dangling and gyrating on its cord in a most suggestive fashion, you notice, pinned to the lapel of a coat here and there, a strip of paper announcing the very low price at which you may become the happy possessor. That dissipates the illusion.

POLONIUS, in the play, gets killed — and not any too soon. If it only were practicable to kill him in real life! A story — to be called The Passing of Polonius — in which a king issues a decree condemning to death every long-winded, didactic person in the kingdom, irrespective of rank, and is himself instantly arrested and decapitated. The man who suspects his own tediousness is yet to be born.

WHENEVER I take up Emerson's poems I find myself turning automatically to his Bacchus. Elsewhere, in detachable passages embedded in mediocre verse, he rises for a moment to heights not reached by any other of our poets; but Bacchus is in the grand style throughout. Its texture can bear comparison with the world's best in this kind. In imaginative quality and austere richness of diction what other verse of our period approaches it? The day Emerson wrote Bacchus he had in him, as Michael Drayton said of Marlowe, " those brave translunary things that the first poets had."

IMAGINE all human beings swept off the face of the earth, excepting one man. Imagine this man in some vast city, New York or London. Imagine him on the third or fourth day of his solitude sitting in a house and hearing a ring at the door-bell!

No man has ever yet succeeded in painting an honest portrait of himself in an autobiography, however sedulously he may have set to work about it. In spite of his candid purpose he omits necessary touches and adds superfluous ones. At times he cannot help draping his thought, and the least shred of drapery becomes a disguise. It is only the diarist who accomplishes the feat of self-portraiture, and he, without any such end in view, does it unconsciously. A man cannot keep a daily record of his comings and goings and the little items that make up the sum of his life, and not inadvertently betray himself at every turn. He lays bare his heart with a candor not possible to the self-consciousness that inevitably colors premeditated revelation. While Pepys was filling those small octavo pages with his perplexing cipher he never once suspected that he was adding a photographic portrait of himself to the world's gallery of immortals. We are more intimately acquainted with Mr. Samuel Pepys, the inner man — his little meannesses and his large generosities — than we are with half the persons we call our dear friends.

THE young girl in my story is to be as sensitive to praise as a prism is to light. Whenever anybody praises her she breaks into colors.

IN the process of dusting my study, the other morning, the maid replaced an engraving of Philip II. of Spain up-side down on the mantel-shelf, and his majesty has remained in that undignified posture ever since. I have no disposition to come to his aid. My abhorrence of the wretch is as hearty as if he had not been dead and — otherwise provided for these last three hundred years. Bloody Mary of England was nearly as merciless, but she was sincere and uncompromising in her extirpation of heretics.

Philip II., whose one recorded hearty laugh was occasioned by the news of the St. Bartholomew massacre, could mask his fanaticism or drop it for the time being, when it seemed politic to do so. Queen Mary was a maniac; but the successor of Torquemada was the incarnation of cruelty pure and simple, and I have a mind to let my counterfeit presentment of him stand on its head for the rest of its natural life. I cordially dislike several persons, but I hate nobody, living or dead, excepting Philip II. of Spain. He appears to give me as much trouble as Charles I. gave the amiable Mr. Dick.

Among the delightful men and women whom you are certain to meet at an English country house there is generally one guest who is supposed to be preternaturally clever and amusing — "so very droll, don't you know." He recites things, tells stories in costermonger dialect, and mimics public characters. He is a type of a class, and I take him to be one of the elementary forms of animal life, like the acalephæ. His presence is capable of adding a gloom to an undertaker's establishment. The last time I fell in with him was on a coaching trip through Devon, and in spite of what I have said I must confess to receiving an instant of entertainment at his hands. He was delivering a little dissertation on "the English and American languages." As there were two Americans on the back seat — it seems we term ourselves "Amurricans" — his choice of subject was full of tact. It was exhilarating to get a lesson in pronunciation from a gentleman who said *boult* for bolt, called St. John *Sin' Jun*, and did not know how to pronounce the beautiful name of his own college at Oxford. Fancy a perfectly sober man saying *Maudlin* for Magdalen! Perhaps the purest English spoken is that of the English folk who have resided abroad ever since the Elizabethan period, or thereabouts.

EVERY one has a bookplate these days, and the collectors are after it. The fool and his book-plate are soon parted. To distribute one's *ex-libris* is inanely to destroy the only significance it has, that of indicating the past or present ownership of the volume in which it is placed.

WHEN an Englishman is not highly imaginative he is apt to be the most matter-of-fact of mortals. He is rarely imaginative, and seldom has an alert sense of humor. Yet England has produced the finest of humorists and the greatest of poets. The humor and imagination which are diffused through other peoples concentrate themselves from time to time in individual Englishmen.

THIS is a page of autobiography, though not written in the first person: Many years ago a noted Boston publisher used to keep a large memorandum-book on a table in his personal office. The volume always lay open, and was in no manner a private affair, being the receptacle of nothing more important than hastily scrawled reminders to attend to this thing or the other. It chanced one day that a very young, unfledged author, passing through the city, looked in upon the publisher, who was also the editor of a famous magazine. The unfledged had a copy of verses secreted about his person. The publisher was absent, and young Milton, feeling that " they also serve who only stand and wait," sat down and waited. Presently his eye fell upon the memorandum-book, lying there spread out like a morning newspaper, and almost in spite of himself he read : " Don't forget to see the binder," " Don't forget to mail E—— his contract," " Don't forget H——'s proofs," etc. An inspiration seized upon the youth ; he took a pencil, and at the tail of this long list of " don't forgets " he wrote : " Don't forget to accept A——'s poem." He left his manuscript on the table and disappeared. That afternoon

14

when the publisher glanced over his memoranda, he was not a little astonished at the last item ; but his sense of humor was so strong that he did accept the poem (it required a strong sense of humor to do that), and sent the lad a check for it, though the verses remain to this day unprinted. That kindly publisher was wise as well as kind.

FRENCH novels with metaphysical or psychological prefaces are always certain to be particularly indecent.

I HAVE lately discovered that Master Harry Sandford of England, the priggish little boy in the story of "Sandford and Merton," has a worthy American cousin in one Elsie Dinsmore, who sedately pirouettes through a seemingly endless succession of girls' books. I came across a nest of fifteen of them the other day. This impossible female is carried from infancy up to grandmotherhood, and is, I believe, still lei-

15

surely pursuing her way down to the tomb in an ecstatic state of uninterrupted didacticism. There are twenty-five volumes of her and the granddaughter, who is also christened Elsie, and is her grandmother's own child, with the same precocious readiness to dispense ethical instruction to her elders. An interesting instance of hereditary talent!

H——'s intellect resembles a bamboo — slender, graceful, and hollow. Personally, he is long and narrow, and looks as if he might have been the product of a rope-walk. He is loosely put together, like an ill-constructed sentence, and affects me like one. His figure is ungrammatical.

AMERICAN humor is nearly as ephemeral as the flowers that bloom in the spring. Each generation has its own crop, and, as a rule, insists on cultivating a new kind. That of 1860, if it were to break into blossom at the present moment, would probably be left to fade upon the stem.

16

Humor is a delicate shrub, with the passing hectic flush of its time. The current-topic variety is especially subject to very early frosts, as is also the dialectic species. Mark Twain's humor is not to be classed with the fragile plants; it has a serious root striking deep down into rich earth, and I think it will go on flowering indefinitely.

I HAVE been imagining an ideal critical journal, whose plan should involve the discharge of the chief literary critic and the installment of a fresh censor on the completion of each issue. To place a man in permanent absolute control of a certain number of pages, in which to express his opinions, is to place him in a position of great personal danger. It is almost inevitable that he should come to overrate the importance of those opinions, to take himself with far too much seriousness, and in the end adopt the dogma of his own infallibility. The liberty to summon this or that man-of-letters to a supposititious bar of justice is apt to beget in the self-appointed judge an exaggerated sense of superiority. He becomes impatient of any rulings not his, and says in effect, if not in so many words : " I am Sir Oracle, and when I ope my lips let no dog bark." When the critic reaches this exalted frame of mind his slight usefulness is gone.

Good

AFTER a debauch of thunder - shower, the weather takes the pledge and signs it with a rainbow.

I LIKE to have a thing suggested rather than told in full. When every detail is given, the mind rests satisfied, and the imagination loses the desire to use its own wings. The partly draped statue has a charm which the nude lacks. Who would have those marble folds slip from the raised knee of the Venus of Melos? Hawthorne knew how to make his lovely thought lovelier by sometimes half veiling it.

I HAVE just tested the nib of a new pen on a slight fancy which Herrick has handled twice in the " Hesperides." The fancy, however, is not Herrick's; it is as old as poetry and the exaggeration of lovers, and I have the same privilege as another to try my fortune with it:

UP ROOS THE SONNE, AND UP ROOS EMELYE

CHAUCER

When some hand has partly drawn
    The cloudy curtains of her bed,
    And my lady's golden head
Glimmers in the dusk like dawn,
Then methinks is day begun.
Later, when her dream has ceased
    And she softly stirs and wakes,
Then it is as when the East
    A sudden rosy magic takes
From the cloud-enfolded sun,
    And full day breaks !

Shakespeare, who has done so much to discourage literature by anticipating everybody, puts the whole matter into a nutshell:

But soft! what light through yonder window breaks?
It is the east, and Juliet is the sun.

19

THERE is a phrase spoken by Hamlet which I have seen quoted innumerable times, and never once correctly. Hamlet, addressing Horatio, says:

> Give me that man
> That is not passion's slave, and I will wear him
> In my heart's core, ay, in my *heart of heart*.

The words italicized are invariably written "heart of hearts" — as if a person possessed that organ in duplicate. Perhaps no one living, with the exception of Sir Henry Irving, is more familiar with the play of Hamlet than my good friend Mr. Bram Stoker, who makes his heart plural on two occasions in his recent novel, "The Mystery of the Sea." Mrs. Humphry Ward also twice misquotes the passage in "Lady Rose's Daughter."

BOOKS that have become classics — books that have had their day and now get more praise than perusal — always remind me of venerable colonels and majors and captains who, having reached the age limit, find themselves retired upon half pay.

WHETHER or not the fretful porcupine rolls itself into a ball is a subject over which my friend John Burroughs and several brother naturalists have lately become as heated as if the question involved points of theology. Up among the Adirondacks, and in the very heart of the region of porcupines, I happen to have a modest cottage. This retreat is called The Porcupine, and I ought by good rights to know something about the habits of the small animal from which it derives its name. Last winter my dog Buster used to return home on an average of three times a month from an excursion up Mt. Pisgah with his nose stuck full of quills, and *he* ought to have some concrete ideas on the subject. We two, then, are prepared to testify that the porcupine in its moments of relaxation occasionally contracts itself into what might be taken for a ball by persons not too difficult to please in the matter of spheres. But neither Buster nor I — being unwilling to get into trouble — would like to assert that it is an actual ball. That it is a shape with which one had better not thoughtlessly meddle is a conviction that my friend Buster stands ready to defend against all comers.

WORDSWORTH'S characterization of the woman in one of his poems as " a creature not too bright or good for human nature's daily food " has always appeared to me too cannibalesque to be poetical. It directly sets one to thinking of the South Sea islanders.

THOUGH Iago was not exactly the kind of person one would select as a superintendent for a Sunday-school, his advice to young Roderigo was wisdom itself — " Put money in thy purse." Whoever disparages money disparages every step in the progress of the human race. I listened the other day to a sermon in which gold was personified as a sort of glittering devil tempting mortals to their ruin. I had an instant of natural hesitation when the contribution-plate was passed around immediately afterward. Personally, I believe that the possession of gold has ruined fewer men than the lack of it. What noble enterprises have been checked and what fine souls have been blighted in the gloom of poverty the world will never know. " After the love of knowledge," says Buckle, " there is no one passion which has done so much good to mankind as the love of money."

DIALECT tempered with slang is an admirable medium of communication between persons who have nothing to say and persons who would not care for anything properly said.

DR. HOLMES had an odd liking for ingenious desk-accessories in the way of pencil-sharpeners, paper-weights, penholders, etc. The latest contrivances in this fashion — probably dropped down to him by the inventor angling for a nibble of commendation — were always making one another's acquaintance on his study table. He once said to me : " I'm waiting for somebody to invent a mucilage-brush that you can't by any accident put into your inkstand. It would save me frequent moments of humiliation."

THE deceptive Mr. False and the volatile Mrs. Giddy, who figure in the pages of seventeenth and eighteenth century fiction, are not tolerated in modern novels and plays. Steal the burglar and Palette the artist have ceased to be. A name indicating the quality or occupation of the bearer strikes us as a too transparent device. Yet there are such names in contemporary real life. That of our worthy Adjutant-General Drum may be instanced. Neal and Pray are a pair of deacons who linger in the memory of my boyhood. Sweet the confectioner and Lamb the butcher are individuals with whom I have had dealings. The old-time sign of Ketchum & Cheetam, Brokers, in Wall Street, New York, seems almost too good to be true. But it was once, if it is not now, an actuality.

I HAVE observed that whenever a Boston author dies, New York immediately becomes a great literary centre.

good

THE possession of unlimited power will make a despot of almost any man. There is a possible Nero in the gentlest human creature that walks.

EVERY living author has a projection of himself, a sort of eidolon, that goes about in near and remote places making friends or enemies for him among persons who never lay eyes upon the writer in the flesh. When he dies, this phantasmal personality fades away, and the author lives only in the impression created by his own literature. It is only then that the world begins

25

to perceive what manner of man the poet, the novelist, or the historian really was. Not until he is dead, and perhaps some long time dead, is it possible for the public to take his exact measure. Up to that point contemporary criticism has either overrated him or underrated him, or ignored him altogether, having been misled by the eidolon, which always plays fantastic tricks with the writer temporarily under its dominion. It invariably represents him as either a greater or a smaller personage than he actually is. Presently the simulacrum works no more spells, good or evil, and the deception is unveiled. The hitherto disregarded author is recognized, and the idol of yesterday, which seemed so important, is taken down from his too large pedestal and carted off to the dumping-ground of inadequate things. To be sure, if he chances to have been not entirely unworthy, and on cool examination is found to possess some appreciable degree of merit, then he is set up on a new slab of appropriate dimensions. The late colossal statue shrinks to a modest bas-relief. On the other hand, some scarcely noticed bust may suddenly become a revered full-length figure. Between the reputation of the author living and the reputation of the same author dead there is ever a wide discrepancy.

A NOT too enchanting glimpse of Tennyson is incidentally given by Charles Brookfield, the English actor, in his " Random Recollections." Mr. Brookfield's father was, on one occasion, dining at the Oxford and Cambridge Club with George Venables, Frank Lushington, Alfred Tennyson, and others. " After dinner," relates the random recollector, " the poet insisted upon putting his feet on the table, tilting back his chair *more Americano*. There were strangers in the room, and he was expostulated with for his uncouthness, but in vain. ' Do put down your feet ! ' pleaded his host. ' Why should I ? ' retorted Tennyson. ' I 'm very comfortable as I am.' ' Every one 's staring at you,' said another. 'Let 'em stare,' replied the poet, placidly. 'Alfred,' said my father, 'people will think you're Longfellow.' Down went the feet." That *more Americano* of Brookfield the younger is delicious with its fine insular flavor, but the holding up of Longfellow — the soul of gentleness, the prince of courtesy — as a bugaboo of bad manners is simply inimitable. It will take England years and years to detect the full unconscious humor of it.

GREAT orators who are not also great writers become very indistinct historical shadows to the generations immediately following them. The spell vanishes with the voice. A man's voice is almost the only part of him entirely obliterated by death. The violet of his native land may be made of his ashes, but nature in her economy seems to have taken no care of his intonations, unless she perpetuates them in restless waves of air surging about the poles. The well-graced actor who leaves no perceptible record of his genius has a decided advantage over the mere orator. The tradition of the player's method and presence is associated with works of enduring beauty. Turning to the pages of the dramatist, we can picture to ourselves the greatness of Garrick or Siddons in this or that scene, in this or that character. It is not so easy to conjure up the impassioned orator from the pages of a dry and possibly illogical argument in favor of or against some long-ago-exploded measure of government. The laurels of an orator who is not a master of literary art wither quickly.

ALL the best sands of my life are somehow getting into the wrong end of the hour-glass. If I could only reverse it! Were it in my power to do so, would I?

SHAKESPEARE is forever coming into our affairs — putting in his oar, so to speak — with some pat word or sentence. The conversation, the other evening, had turned on the subject of

29

watches, when one of the gentlemen present, the manager of a large watch-making establishment, told us a rather interesting fact. The component parts of a watch are produced by different workmen, who have no concern with the complex piece of mechanism as a whole, and possibly, as a rule, understand it imperfectly. Each worker needs to be expert in only his own special branch. When the watch has reached a certain advanced state, the work requires a touch as delicate and firm as that of an oculist performing an operation. Here the most skilled and trustworthy artisans are employed; they receive high wages, and have the benefit of a singular indulgence. In case the workman, through too continuous application, finds himself lacking the steadiness of nerve demanded by his task, he is allowed without forfeiture of pay to remain idle temporarily, in order that his hand may recover the requisite precision of touch. As I listened, Hamlet's courtly criticism of the grave-digger's want of

30

sensibility came drifting into my memory. " The hand of little employment hath the daintier sense," says Shakespeare, who has left nothing unsaid.

It was a festival in honor of **Dai Butsu** or some one of the auxiliary deities that preside over the destinies of Japland. For three days and nights the streets of Tokio — where the squat little brown houses look for all the world as if they were mimicking the favorite sitting posture of the Japanese — were crowded with smiling holiday makers, and made gay with devices of tinted tissue paper, dolphins, devils, dragons, and mythical winged creatures which at night amiably turned themselves into lanterns. Garlands of these, arranged close together, were stretched across the streets from ridgepole to ridgepole, and your jinrikisha whisked you through interminable arbors of soft illumination. The spectacle gave one an idea of fairyland, but then all Japan does that.

31

A land not like ours, that land of strange flowers,
Of dæmons and spooks with mysterious powers —
　Of gods who breathe ice, who cause peach-blooms and rice
And manage the moonshine and turn on the showers.

Each day has its fair or its festival there,
And life seems immune to all trouble and care —
　Perhaps only seems, in that island of dreams,
Sea-girdled and basking in magical air.

They 've streets of bazaars filled with lacquers and jars,
And silk stuffs, and sword-blades that tell of old wars;
　They 've Fuji's white cone looming up, bleak and lone,
As if it were trying to reach to the stars.

They 've temples and gongs, and grim Buddhas in throngs,
And pearl-powdered geisha with dances and songs:
　Each girl at her back has an imp, brown or black,
And dresses her hair in remarkable prongs.

On roadside and street toddling images meet,
And smirk and kotow in a way that is sweet;
　Their obis are tied with particular pride,
Their silken kimonos hang scant to the feet.

With purrs like a cat they all giggle and chat,
Now spreading their fans, and now holding them flat;
　A fan by its play whispers, " Go now ! " or " Stay ! "
" I hate you ! " " I love you ! " — a fan can say that !

32

Beneath a dwarf tree, here and there, two or three
Squat coolies are sipping small cups of green tea;
   They sputter, and leer, and cry out, and appear
Like bad little chessmen gone off on a spree.

At night — ah, at night the long streets are a sight,
With garlands of soft-colored lanterns alight —
   Blue, yellow, and red twinkling high overhead,
Like thousands of butterflies taking their flight.

Somewhere in the gloom that no lanterns illume
Stand groups of slim lilies and jonquils in bloom;
   On tiptoe, unseen 'mid a tangle of green,
They offer the midnight their cups of perfume.

At times, sweet and clear from some tea-garden near,
A ripple of laughter steals out to your ear;
   Anon the wind brings from a samisen's strings
The pathos that 's born of a smile and a tear.

THE difference between an English audience
and a French audience at the theatre is marked.
The Frenchman brings down a witticism on the
wing. The Briton pauses for it to alight and
give him reasonable time for deliberate aim. In
English playhouses an appreciable number of
seconds usually precede the smile or the ripple

of laughter that follows a facetious turn of the least fineness. I disclaim all responsibility for this statement of my personal observation, since it has recently been indorsed by one of London's most eminent actors.

At the next table, taking his opal drops of absinthe, was a French gentleman with the blasé aspect of an empty champagne-bottle, which always has the air of saying: "I have lived!"

WE often read of wonderful manifestations of memory, but they are always instances of the faculty working in some special direction. It is memory playing, like Paganini, on one string. No doubt the persons performing the phenomenal feats ascribed to them have forgotten more than they remember. To be able to repeat a hundred lines of verse after a single reading is no proof of a retentive mind, excepting so far as the hundred lines go. A man might easily fail under such a test, and yet have a good memory; by which I mean a catholic one, and that I imagine to be nearly the rarest of gifts. I have never met more than four or five persons possessing it. The small boy who defined memory as " the thing you forget with " described the faculty as it exists and works in the majority of men and women.

THE survival in publishers of the imitative instinct is a strong argument in support of Mr. Darwin's theory of the descent of man. One publisher no sooner brings out a new style of book-cover than half a dozen other publishers fall to duplicating it.

THE cavalry sabre hung over the chimney-place with a knot of violets tied to the dinted guard, there being no known grave to decorate. For many a year, on each Decoration Day, a sorrowful woman had come and fastened these flowers there. The first time she brought her offering

35

she was a slender girl, as fresh as her own violets. It is a slender figure still, but there are
threads of silver in the black hair.

FORTUNATE was Marcus Aurelius Antoninus,
who in early youth was taught " to abstain from
rhetoric, and poetry, and fine writing " — especially the fine writing. Simplicity is art's last
word.

THE man is clearly an adventurer. In the seventeenth century he would have worn huge flint-
lock pistols stuck into a wide leather belt, and
been something in the seafaring line. The fellow is always smartly dressed, but where he
lives and how he lives are as unknown as
" what song the Sirens sang, or what name
Achilles assumed when he hid himself among
women." He is a man who apparently has no
appointment with his breakfast and whose dinner is a chance acquaintance. His probable
banker is the next person. A great city like

this is the only geography for such a character. He would be impossible in a small country town, where everybody knows everybody and what everybody has for lunch.

I HAVE been seeking, thus far in vain, for the proprietor of the saying that "Economy is second or third cousin to Avarice." I went rather confidently to Rochefoucauld, but it is not among that gentleman's light luggage of cynical maxims.

THERE is a popular vague impression that butchers are not allowed to serve as jurors on murder trials. This is not really the case, but it logically might be. To a man daily familiar with the lurid incidents of the *abattoir*, the summary extinction of a fellow creature (whether the victim or the criminal) can scarcely seem a circumstance of so serious moment as to another man engaged in less strenuous pursuits.

37

WE do not, and cannot, read many of the novels that most delighted our ancestors. Some of our popular fiction is doubtless as poor, but poor with a difference. There is always a heavy demand for fresh mediocrity. In every generation the least cultivated taste has the largest appetite. There is ragtime literature as well as ragtime music for the many.

G—— is a man who had rather fail in a great purpose than not accomplish it in precisely his own way. He has the courage of his conviction and the intolerance of his courage. He is opposed to the death penalty for murder, but he would willingly have any one electrocuted who disagreed with him on the subject.

I HAVE thought of an essay to be called "On the Art of Short-Story Writing," but have given it up as smacking too much of the shop. It would be too *intime*, since I should have to deal

38

chiefly with my own ways, and so give myself the false air of seeming to consider them of importance. It would interest nobody to know that I always write the last paragraph first, and then work directly up to that, avoiding all digressions and side issues. Then who on earth would care to be told about the trouble my characters cause me by talking too much? They *will* talk, and I have to let them; but when the story is finished, I go over the dialogue and strike out four fifths of the long speeches. I fancy that makes my characters pretty mad.

THIS is the golden age of the inventor. He is no longer looked upon as a madman or a wizard, incontinently to be made away with. Two or three centuries ago Marconi would not have escaped a ropeless end with his wireless telegraphy. Even so late as 1800, the friends of one Robert Fulton seriously entertained the luminous idea of hustling the poor man into an asy-

lum for the unsound before he had a chance to
fire up the boiler of his tiny steamboat on the
Hudson river. In olden times the pillory and
the whipping-post were among the gentler forms
of encouragement awaiting the inventor. If a
man devised an especially practical apple-peeler
he was in imminent danger of being peeled with
it by an incensed populace. To-day we hail
with enthusiasm a scientific or a mechanical
discovery, and stand ready to make a stock
company of it.

A MAN is known by the company his mind
keeps. To live continually with noble books,
with " high-erected thoughts seated in the heart
of courtesy," teaches the soul good manners.

THE unconventional has ever a morbid attrac-
tion for a certain class of mind. There is always
a small coterie of highly intellectual men and
women eager to give welcome to whatever is
eccentric, obscure, or chaotic. Worshipers at

the shrine of the Unpopular, they tingle with a sense of tolerant superiority when they say: "Of course this is not the kind of thing *you* would like." Sometimes these impressionable souls almost seem to make a sort of reputation for their fetish.

I HEAR that B—— directed to have himself buried on the edge of the pond where his duck-stand was located, in order that flocks of migrating birds might fly over his grave every autumn. He did not have to die, to become a dead shot. A comrade once said of him: "Yes, B—— is a great sportsman. He has peppered everything from grouse in North Dakota to his best friend in the Maine woods."

WHEN the novelist introduces a bore into his novel he must not let him bore the reader. The fellow must be made amusing, which he would not be in real life. In nine cases out of ten an exact reproduction of real life would prove tedious. Facts are not necessarily valuable, and frequently they add nothing to fiction. The art of the realistic novelist sometimes seems akin to that of the Chinese tailor who perpetuated the old patch on the new trousers. True art selects and paraphrases, but seldom gives a verbatim translation.

THE last meeting I had with Lowell was in the north room of his house at Elmwood, the sleeping-room I had occupied during a two years' tenancy of the place in his absence abroad. He was lying half propped up in bed, convalescing from one of the severe attacks that were ultimately to prove fatal. Near the bed was a chair on which stood a marine picture in aquarelle — a stretch of calm sea, a bit of rocky shore in the foreground, if I remember, and a vessel at anchor. The afternoon sunlight, falling through the window, cast a bloom over the picture, which was turned toward Lowell. From time to time, as he spoke, his eyes rested thoughtfully on the water-color. A friend, he said, had just sent it to him. It seemed to me then, and the fancy has often haunted me since, that that ship, in the golden haze, with top-sails loosened, was waiting to bear his spirit away.

CIVILIZATION is the lamb's skin in which barbarism masquerades. If somebody has already said that, I forgive him the mortification he causes me. At the beginning of the twentieth century barbarism can throw off its gentle disguise, and burn a man at the stake as complacently as in the Middle Ages.

WHAT is slang in one age sometimes goes into the vocabulary of the purist in the next. On the other hand, expressions that once were not considered inelegant are looked at askance in the period following. The word " brass " was formerly an accepted synonym for money; but at present, when it takes on that significance, it is not admitted into genteel circles of language. It may be said to have seen better days, like another word I have in mind — a word that has become slang, employed in the sense which once did not exclude it from very good society. A friend lately informed me that he had " fired " his housekeeper — that is, dismissed her. He little dreamed that he was speaking excellent Elizabethan.

THE " Journal des Goncourt " is crowded with beautiful and hideous things, like a Japanese Museum.

" AND she shuddered as she sat, still silent, on her seat, and he saw that she shuddered." This is from Anthony Trollope's novel, " Can You Forgive Her? " Can you forgive him? is the next question.

A LITTLE thing may be perfect, but perfection is not a little thing. Possessing this quality, a trifle "no bigger than an agate-stone on the forefinger of an alderman" shall outlast the Pyramids. The world will have forgotten all the great masterpieces of literature when it forgets Lovelace's three verses to Lucasta on his going to the wars. More durable than marble or bronze are the words, "I could not love thee, deare, so much, loved I not honor more."

I CALLED on the dear old doctor this afternoon to say good-by. I shall probably not find him here when I come back from the long voyage which I have in front of me. He is very fragile, and looks as though a puff of wind would blow him away. He said himself, with his old-time cheerfulness, that he was attached to this earth by only a little piece of twine. He has perceptibly failed since I saw him a month ago; but he was full of the wise and radiant talk to which all the world has listened, and will miss. I found him absorbed in a newly made card-catalogue of his library. "It was absurd of me to

45

have it done," he remarked. "What I really require is a little bookcase holding only two volumes; then I could go from one to the other in alternation and always find each book as fresh as if I never had read it." This arraignment of his memory was in pure jest, for the doctor's mind was to the end like an unclouded crystal. It was interesting to note how he studied himself, taking his own pulse, as it were, and diagnosing his own case in a sort of scientific, impersonal way, as if it were somebody else's case and he were the consulting specialist. I intended to spend a quarter of an hour with him, and he kept me three hours. I went there rather depressed, but I returned home leavened with his good spirits, which, I think, will never desert him, here or hereafter. To keep the heart unwrinkled, to be hopeful, kindly, cheerful, reverent — that is to triumph over old age.

THE thing one reads and likes, and then forgets, is of no account. The thing that stays, and haunts one, and refuses to be forgotten, that is the sincere thing. I am describing the impression left upon me by Mr. Howells's blank-verse sketch called "Father and Mother: A Mystery" — a strangely touching and imaginative piece of work, not unlike in effect to some of Maeterlinck's psychical dramas. As I read on, I seemed to be standing in a shadow cast by some half-remembered experience of my own in a previous state of existence. When I went to bed that night I had to lie awake and think it over as an event that had actually befallen me. I should call the effect *weird*, if the word had not lately been worked to death. The gloom of Poe and the spirituality of Hawthorne touch cold finger-tips in those three or four pages.

For a character-study — a man made up entirely of limitations. His conservatism and negative qualities to be represented as causing him to attain success where men of conviction and real ability fail of it.

47

A DARK, saturnine man sat opposite me at table on board the steamer. During the entire run from Sandy Hook to Fastnet Light he addressed no one at meal-times excepting his table steward. Seated next to him, on the right, was a vivacious gentleman, who, like Gratiano in the play, spoke " an infinite deal of nothing." He made persistent and pathetic attempts to lure his silent neighbor (we had christened him " William the Silent ") into conversation, but a monosyllable was always the poor result — until one day. It was the last day of the voyage. We had stopped at the entrance to Queenstown harbor to deliver the mails, and some fish had been brought aboard. The vivacious gentleman was in a high state of excitement that morning at table. " Fresh fish ! " he exclaimed ; " actually fresh ! They seem quite different from ours. Irish fish, of course. Can you tell me, sir," he inquired, turning to his gloomy shipmate, " what *kind* of fish these are ? " " Cork soles," said the saturn-

ine man, in a deep voice, and then went on
with his breakfast.

LOWELL used to find food for great mirth in
General George P. Morris's line,

> Her heart and morning broke together.

Lowell's well-beloved Dr. Donne, however,
had an attack of the same platitude, and possibly inoculated poor Morris. Even literature
seems to have its mischief-making bacilli. The
late " incomparable and ingenious Dean of St.
Paul's " says,

> The day breaks not, it is my heart.

I think Dr. Donne's case rather worse than
Morris's. Chaucer had the malady in a milder
form when he wrote :

> Up roos the sonne, and up roos Emelye.

The charming naïveté of it !

SITTING in Ellen Terry's dressing-room at the
Lyceum Theatre one evening during that lady's
temporary absence on the stage, Sarah Bern-

hardt picked up a crayon and wrote this pretty word on the mirror — *Dearling*, mistaking it for the word darling. The French actress lighted by chance upon a Spenserianism now become obsolete without good reason. It is a more charming adjective than the one that has replaced it.

A DEAD author appears to be bereft of all earthly rights. He is scarcely buried before old magazines and newspapers are ransacked in search of matters which, for reasons sufficient to him, he had carefully excluded from the definitive edition of his collected writings.

> He gave the people of his best;
> His worst he kept, his best he gave.

One can imagine a poet tempted to address some such appeal as this to any possible future publisher of his poems :

> Take what thou wilt, a lyric or a line,
> Take all, take nothing — and God send thee cheer!
> But my anathema on thee and thine
> If thou add'st aught to what is printed here.

THE claim of this country to call itself "The Land of the Free" must be held in abeyance until every man in it, whether he belongs or does not belong to a labor organization, shall have the right to work for his daily bread.

THERE is a strain of primitive poetry running through the entire Irish race, a fleeting lyrical emotion which expresses itself in a flash, usually in connection with love of country and kindred across the sea. I had a touching illustration of it the other morning. The despot who reigns over our kitchen was gathering a mess of dandelions on the rear lawn. It was one of those blue and gold days which seem especially to belong to New England. "It's in County Westmeath I'd be this day," she said, looking up at me. "*I'd go cool my hands in the grass on my ould mother's grave in the bit of churchyard foreninst the priest's house at Mullingar.*" I have seen poorer poetry than that in the magazines.

51

Speaking of the late Major Pond, the well-known director of a lecture bureau, an old client of his remarked : " He was a most capable manager, but it always made me a little sore to have him deduct twenty-five per cent. commission." " Pond's Extract," murmured one of the gentlemen present.

Each of our great towns has its " Little Italy," with shops where nothing is spoken but Italian and streets in which the alien pedestrian had better not linger after nightfall. The chief industry of these exotic communities seems to be spaghetti and stilettos. What with our Little Italys and Chinatowns, and the like, an American need not cross the ocean in order to visit foreign lands and enjoy the benefits of older civilizations.

Poets are made as well as born, the proverb notwithstanding. They are made possible by the general love of poetry and the consequent imperious demand for it. When this is non-existent, poets become mute, the atmosphere stifles them. There would have been no Shakespeare had there been no Elizabethan audience. That was an age when, as Emerson finely puts it,

> Men became
> Poets, for the air was fame.

THE stolid gentleman in livery who has his carriage-stand at the corner opposite my house is constantly touching on the extremes of human experience, with probably not the remotest perception of the fact. Now he takes a pair of lovers out for an airing, and now he drives the absconding bank-teller to the railway-station. Excepting as question of distance, the man has positively no choice between a theatre and a graveyard. I met him this morning dashing up to the portals of Trinity Church with a bridal party, and this afternoon, as I was crossing Cambridge Bridge, I saw him creeping along next to the hearse, on

53

his way to Mount Auburn. The wedding afforded him no pleasure, and the funeral gave him no grief; yet he was a factor in both. It is his odd destiny to be wholly detached from the vital part of his own acts. If the carriage itself could speak! The autobiography of a public hack written without reservation would be dramatic reading.

In this blotted memorandum-book are a score or two of suggestions for essays, sketches, and poems, which I have not written, and never shall write. The instant I jot down an idea the desire to utilize it leaves me, and I turn away to do something unpremeditated. The shabby volume has become a sort of Potter's Field where I bury my literary intentions, good and bad, without any belief in their final resurrection.

A STAGE-direction: *Exit Time; enter Eternity — with a soliloquy.*

ASIDES

TOM FOLIO

IN my early Boston days a gentle soul was often to be met with about town, furtively haunting old book-shops and dusty editorial rooms, a man of ingratiating simplicity of manner, who always spoke in a low, hesitating voice, with a note of refinement in it. He was a devout worshiper of Elia, and wrote pleasant discursive essays smacking somewhat of his master's flavor — suggesting rather than imitating it — which he signed " Tom Folio." I forget how he glided into my acquaintanceship; doubtless in some way too shy and elusive for remembrance. I never knew him intimately, perhaps no one did, but the intercourse between us was most cordial, and our chance meetings and bookish chats extended over a space of a dozen years.

Tom Folio — I cling to the winning pseu-
donym — was sparely built and under medium
height, or maybe a slight droop of the shoulders
made it seem so, with a fragile look about him
and an aspect of youth that was not his. En-
countering him casually on a street corner, you
would, at the first glance, have taken him for a
youngish man, but the second glance left you
doubtful. It was a figure that struck a note of
singularity and would have attracted your attention even in a crowd.

During the first four or five years of our acquaintance, meeting him only out of doors or in
shops, I had never happened to see him with his
hat off. One day he recklessly removed it, and
in the twinkling of an eye he became an elderly
bald-headed man. The Tom Folio I once knew
had virtually vanished. An instant earlier he
was a familiar shape; an instant later, an almost
unrecognizable individual. A narrow fringe of
light-colored hair, extending from ear to ear
under the rear brim of his hat, had perpetrated

an unintentional deception by leading one to sup-
pose a head profusely covered with curly locks.
" Tom Folio," I said, " put on your hat and
come back ! " But after that day he never seemed
young to me.

I had few or no inklings of his life disconnected with the streets and the book-stalls, chiefly
those on Cornhill or in the vicinity. It is possible I am wrong in inferring that he occupied a
room somewhere at the South End or in South
Boston, and lived entirely alone, heating his cof-
fee and boiling his egg over an alcohol lamp. I
got from him one or two fortuitous hints of
quaint housekeeping. Every winter, it appeared,
some relative, far or near, sent him a large batch
of mince pies, twenty or thirty at least. He once
spoke to me of having laid in his winter pie, just
as another might speak of laying in his winter
coal. The only fireside companion Tom Folio
ever alluded to in my presence was a Maltese
cat, whose poor health seriously disturbed him
from time to time. I suspected those mince

pies. The cat, I recollect, was named Miss Mowcher.

If he had any immediate family ties beyond this I was unaware of them, and not curious to be enlightened on the subject. He was more picturesque solitary. I preferred him to remain so. Other figures introduced into the background of the canvas would have spoiled the artistic effect.

Tom Folio was a cheerful, lonely man — a recluse even when he allowed himself to be jostled and hurried along on the turbulent stream of humanity sweeping in opposite directions through Washington Street and its busy estuaries. He was in the crowd, but not of it. I had so little real knowledge of him that I was obliged to imagine his more intimate environments. However wide of the mark my conjectures may have fallen, they were as satisfying to me as facts would have been. His secluded room I could picture to myself with a sense of certainty — the couch (a sofa by day), the cupboard, the writing-table with its student lamp,

the litter of pamphlets and old quartos and oc-
tavos in tattered bindings, among which were
scarce reprints of his beloved Charles Lamb,
and perhaps — nay, surely — an *editio prin-
ceps* of the " Essays."

The gentle Elia never had a gentler follower
or a more loving disciple than Tom Folio. He
moved and had much of his being in the early
part of the last century. To him the South-Sea
House was the most important edifice on the
globe, remaining the same venerable pile it used
to be, in spite of all the changes that had befallen it. It was there Charles Lamb passed the
novitiate of his long years of clerkship in the
East India Company. In Tom Folio's fancy a
slender, boyish figure was still seated, quill in
hand, behind those stately porticoes looking upon
Threadneedle Street and Bishopsgate. That
famous first paper in the " Essays," describing
the South-Sea House and the group of human
oddities which occupied desks within its gloomy
chambers, had left an indelible impression upon

the dreamer. Every line traced by the "lean annuitant" was as familiar to Tom Folio as if he had written it himself. Stray scraps, which had escaped the vigilance of able editors, were known to him, and it was his to unearth amid a heap of mouldy, worm-eaten magazines, a handful of leaves hitherto forgotten of all men. Trifles, yes — but Charles Lamb's! "The king's chaff is as good as other people's corn," says Tom Folio.

Often his talk was sweet and racy with old-fashioned phrases; the talk of a man who loved books and drew habitual breath in an atmosphere of fine thought. Next to Charles Lamb, but at a convenable distance, Izaak Walton was Tom Folio's favorite. His poet was Alexander Pope, though he thought Mr. Addison's tragedy of "Cato" contained some proper good lines. Our friend was a wide reader in English classics, greatly preferring the literature of the earlier periods to that of the Victorian age. His smiling, tenderly expressed disapprobation of various

modern authors was enchanting. John Keats's
verses were monstrous pretty, but over-orna-
mented. A little too much lucent syrup tinct
with cinnamon, don't you think? The poetry
of Shelley might have been composed in the
moon by a slightly deranged, well-meaning person. If you wanted a sound mind in a sound
metrical body, why there was Mr. Pope's "Essay
on Man." There was something winsome and
by-gone in the general make-up of Tom Folio.
No man living in the world ever seemed to me
to live so much out of it, or to live more comfortably.

At times I half suspected him of a conva-
lescent amatory disappointment. Perhaps long
before I knew him he had taken a little senti-
mental journey, the unsuccessful end of which
had touched him with a gentle sadness. It was
something far off and softened by memory. If
Tom Folio had any love-affair on hand in my
day, it must have been of an airy, platonic sort
— a chaste secret passion for Mistress Peg Wof-

fington or Nell Gwyn, or possibly Mr. Waller's Saccharissa.

Although Tom Folio was not a collector — that means dividends and bank balances — he had a passion for the Past and all its belongings, with a virtuoso's knowledge of them. A fan painted by Vanloo, a bit of rare Nankin (he had caught from Charles Lamb the love of old china), or an undoctored stipple of Bartolozzi, gave him delight in the handling, though he might not aspire to ownership. I believe he would willingly have drunk any horrible decoction from a silver teapot of Queen Anne's time. These things were not for him in a coarse, materialistic sense; in a spiritual sense he held possession of them in fee-simple. I learned thus much of his tastes one day during an hour we spent together in the rear showroom of a dealer in antiquities.

I have spoken of Tom Folio as lonely, but I am inclined to think that I mis-stated it. He had hosts of friends who used to climb the rather steep staircase leading to that modest third-story

64

front room which I have imagined for him — a room with Turkey-red curtains, I like to believe, and a rare engraving of a scene from Mr. Hogarth's excellent moral of " The Industrious and Idle Apprentices " pinned against the chimney breast. Young Chatterton, who was not always the best of company, dropped in at intervals. There Mr. Samuel Pepys had a special chair reserved for him by the window, where he could catch a glimpse of the pretty housemaid over the way, chatting with the policeman at the area railing. Dr. Johnson and the unworldly author of " The Deserted Village " were frequent visitors, sometimes appearing together arm-in-arm, with James Boswell, Esq., of Auchinleck, following obsequiously behind. Not that Tom Folio did not have callers vastly more aristocratic, though he could have had none pleasanter or wholesomer. Sir Philip Sidney (who must have given Folio that copy of the " Arcadia "), the Viscount St. Albans, and even two or three others before whom either of these might have doffed his bonnet, did not disdain to gather round that hearthstone. Fielding, Smollett, Sterne, Defoe, Dick Steele, Dean Swift — there was no end to them! On certain nights, when all the stolid neighborhood was lapped in slumber, the narrow street stretching beneath Tom Folio's windows must have been blocked with invisible coaches and sedan-chairs, and illuminated by the visionary glare of torches borne by shadowy linkboys hurrying hither and thither. A man so sought after and companioned cannot be described as lonely.

My memory here recalls the fact that he had a few friends less insubstantial — that quaint anatomy perched on the top of a hand-organ, to whom Tom Folio was wont to give a bite of his apple; and the brown-legged little Neapolitan who was always nearly certain of a copper when this multi-millionaire strolled through the slums on a Saturday afternoon — Saturday probably being the essayist's pay-day. The withered woman of the peanut-stand on the corner over against Faneuil Hall Market knew him for a friend, as did also the blind lead-pencil merchant, whom Tom Folio, on occasions, safely piloted across the stormy traffic of Dock Square. *Noblesse oblige!* He was no stranger in those purlieus. Without designing to confuse small things with great, I may say that a certain strip of pavement in North Street could be pointed out as Tom Folio's Walk, just as Addison's Walk is pointed out on the banks of the Cherwell at Oxford.

I used to observe that when Tom Folio was not in quest of a print or a pamphlet or some such urgent thing, but was walking for mere recreation, he instinctively avoided respectable latitudes. He liked best the squalid, ill-kept thoroughfares shadowed by tall, smudgy tenement-houses and teeming with unprosperous, noisy life. Perhaps he had, half consciously, a sense of subtle kinship to the unsuccess and cheerful resignation of it all.

Returning home from abroad one October

67

morning several years ago, I was told that that simple spirit had passed on. His death had been little heeded ; but in him had passed away an intangible genuine bit of Old Boston — as genuine a bit, in its kind, as the Autocrat himself — a personality not to be restored or replaced. Tom Folio could never happen again !

Strolling to-day through the streets of the older section of the town, I miss many a venerable landmark submerged in the rising tide of change, but I miss nothing quite so much as I do the sight of Tom Folio entering the doorway of the Old Corner Bookstore, or carefully taking down a musty volume from its shelf at some melancholy old book-stall on Cornhill.

FLEABODY AND OTHER QUEER NAMES

WHEN an English novelist does us the honor to introduce any of our country-men into his fiction, he generally displays a commendable desire to present something typi-cal in the way of names for his adopted char-acters — to give a dash of local color, as it were, with his nomenclature. His success is seldom commensurate to the desire. He falls into the error of appealing to his invention, instead of consulting some city directory, in which he would find more material than he could exhaust in ten centuries. Charles Reade might have secured in the pages of such a compendium a happier title than Fullalove for his Yankee sea-captain; though I doubt, on the whole, if Anthony Trollope could have discovered anything better than Olivia Q. Fleabody for the young woman from " the States " in his novel called " Is He Popenjoy ? "

To christen a sprightly young female advocate of woman's rights Olivia Q. Fleabody was very happy indeed ; to be candid, it was much better than was usual with Mr. Trollope, whose understanding of American life and manners was not enlarged by extensive travel in this country. An English tourist's preconceived idea of us is a thing he brings over with him on the steamer and carries home again intact ; it is as much a part of his indispensable impedimenta as his hat-box. But Fleabody is excellent ; it was probably suggested by Peabody, which may have struck Mr. Trollope as comical (just as Trollope strikes *us* as comical), or, at least, as not serious. What a capital name Veronica Trollope would be for a hoydenish young woman in a society novel ! I fancy that all foreign names are odd to the alien. I remember that the signs above shop-doors in England and on the Continent used to amuse me often enough, when I was over there. It is a notable circumstance that extraordinary names never seem extraordinary to the persons bearing them. If a fellow-creature were branded Ebenezer Cuttlefish he would remain to the end of his days quite unconscious of anything out of the common.

I am aware that many of our American names are sufficiently queer; but English writers make merry over them, as if our most eccentric were not thrown into the shade by some of their own. No American, living or dead, can surpass the verbal infelicity of Knatchbull-Hugessen, for example — if the gentleman will forgive me for conscripting him. Quite as remarkable, in a grimly significant way, is the appellation of a British officer who was fighting the Boers in the Transvaal in the year of blessed memory 1899. This young soldier, who highly distinguished himself on the field, was known to his brothers-in-arms as Major Pine Coffin. I trust that the gallant major became a colonel later and is still

71

alive. It would eclipse the gayety of nations to lose a man with a name like that.

Several years ago I read in the sober police reports of "The Pall Mall Gazette" an account of a young man named George F. Onions, who was arrested (it ought to have been by "a peeler") for purloining money from his employers, Messrs. Joseph Pickles & Son, stuff merchants, of Bradford — *des noms bien idylliques!* What mortal could have a more ludicrous name than Onions, unless it were Pickles, or Pickled Onions? And then for Onions to rob Pickles! Could there be a more incredible coincidence? As a coincidence it is nearly sublime. No story-writer would dare to present that fact or those names in his fiction; neither would be accepted as possible. Meanwhile Olivia Q. Fleabody is *ben trovato.*

A NOTE ON "L'AIGLON"

THE night-scene on the battlefield of Wagram in " L'Aiglon "— an episode whose
sharp pathos pierces the heart and the imagination like the point of a rapier — bears a striking
resemblance to a picturesque passage in Victor
Hugo's " Les Misérables."   It is the one intense
great moment in the play, and has been widely
discussed, but so far as I am aware none of M.
Rostand's innumerable critics has touched on the
resemblance mentioned.   In the master's romance it is not the field of Wagram, but the
field of Waterloo, that is magically repeopled
with contending armies of spooks, to use the
grim old Dutch word, and made vivid to the
mind's eye.   The passage occurs at the end
of the sixteenth chapter in the second part of

"Les Misérables" (Cosette), and runs as follows:

Le champ de Waterloo aujourd'hui a le calme qui appartient à la terre, support impassible de l'homme, et il resemble à toutes les plaines. La nuit pourtant une espèce de brume visionnaire s'en dégage, et si quelque voyageur s'y promène, s'il regarde, s'il écoute, s'il rêve comme Virgile dans les funestes plaines de Philippes, l'hallucination de la catastrophe le saisit. L'effrayant 18 juin revit; la fausse colline-monument s'efface, ce lion quelconque se dissipe, le champ de bataille reprend sa réalité; des lignes d'infanterie ondulent dans la plaine, des galops furieux traversent l'horizon; le songeur effaré voit l'éclair des sabres, l'étincelle des bayonnettes, le flamboiement des bombes, l'entre-croisement monstrueux des tonnerres; il entend, comme un râle au fond d'une tombe, la clameur vague de la bataille-fantôme; ces ombres, ce sont les grenadiers; ces lueurs, ce sont les cuirassiers; . . . tout cela n'est plus et se heurte et combat encore; et les ravins s'empourprent, et les arbres frissonnent, et il y a de la furie jusque dans les nuées, et, dans les ténèbres, toutes ces hauteurs farouches, Mont-Saint-Jean, Hougomont, Frischemont, Papelotte, Plance-

noit, apparaissent confusément couronnées de tour-
billons de spectres s'exterminant.[1]

Here is the whole battle scene in " L'Aiglon,"
with scarcely a gruesome detail omitted. The
vast plain glimmering in phantasmal light; the
ghostly squadrons hurling themselves against

---

[1] The field of Waterloo has to-day the peacefulness which belongs to earth, the impassive support of man, and is like all other
plains. At night, however, a kind of visionary mist is exhaled,
and if any traveler walks there, and watches and listens, and
dreams like Virgil on the sorrowful plains of Philippi, the hallucination of the catastrophe takes possession of him. The terrible
June 18 relives; the artificial commemorative mound effaces itself,
the lion disappears, the field of battle assumes its reality; lines
of infantry waver on the plain, the horizon is broken by furious
charges of cavalry; the alarmed dreamer sees the gleam of sabres,
the glimmer of bayonets, the lurid glare of bursting shells, the
clashing of mighty thunderbolts; the muffled clamor of the
phantom conflict comes to him like dying moans from the tomb;
these shadows are grenadiers, these lights are cuirassiers . . . all
this does not really exist, yet the combat goes on; the ravines are
stained with purple, the trees tremble, there is fury even in the
clouds, and in the obscurity the sombre heights — Mont-Saint-
Jean, Hougomont, Frischemont, Papelotte, and Plancenoit — appear dimly crowned with throngs of apparitions annihilating one
another.

one another (seen only through the eyes of the poor little Duke of Reichstadt) ; the mangled shapes lying motionless in various postures of death upon the blood-stained sward ; the moans of the wounded rising up and sweeping by like vague wailings of the wind — all this might be taken for an artful appropriation of Victor Hugo's text; but I do not think it was, though it is possible that a faint reflection of a brilliant page, read in early youth, still lingered on the retina of M. Rostand's memory. If such were the case, it does not necessarily detract from the integrity of the conception or the playwright's presentment of it.

The idea of repeopling old battlefields with the shades of vanished hosts is not novel. In such tragic spots the twilight always lays a dark hand on the imagination, and prompts one to invoke the unappeased spirit of the past that haunts the place. One summer evening long ago, as I was standing alone by the ruined walls of Hougomont, with that sense of not being alone which is sometimes so strangely stirred by solitude, I had a sudden vision of that desperate last charge of Napoleon's Old Guard. Marshal Ney rose from the grave and again shouted those heroic words to Drouet d'Erlon: " Are you not going to get yourself killed? " For an instant a thousand sabres flashed in the air. The deathly silence that accompanied the ghostly onset was an added poignancy to the short-lived dream. A moment later I beheld a hunched little figure mounted on a white horse with housings of purple velvet. The reins lay slack in the rider's hand; his three-cornered hat was slouched over his brows, and his chin rested on the breast of his great-coat. Thus he slowly rode away through the twilight, and nobody cried, *Vive l'Empereur!*

The ground on which a famous battle has been fought casts a spell upon every man's . mind; and the impression made upon two men of poetic genius, like Victor Hugo and Edmond Rostand, might well be nearly identical. This sufficiently explains the likeness between the fantastic silhouette in " Les Misérables " and the battle of the ghosts in " L'Aiglon." A muse so rich in the improbable as M. Rostand's need not borrow a piece of supernaturalness from anybody.

PLOT AND CHARACTER

HENRY JAMES, in his paper on Anthony
Trollope, says that if Trollope " had taken
sides on the rather superficial opposition between
novels of character and novels of plot, I can
imagine him to have said (except that he never
expressed himself in epigram) that he preferred
the former class, inasmuch as character in itself
is plot, while plot is by no means character."
So neat an antithesis would surely never have
found itself between Mr. Trollope's lips if Mr.
James had not cunningly lent it to him. Whatever theory of novel-writing Mr. Trollope may
have preached, his almost invariable practice
was to have a plot. He always had a *story* to
tell, and a story involves beginning, middle, and
end — in short, a framework of some description.

There have been delightful books filled wholly

with character-drawing; but they have not been great novels. The great novel deals with human action as well as with mental portraiture and analysis. That "character in itself is plot" is true only in a limited sense. A plan, a motive with a logical conclusion, is as necessary to a novel or a romance as it is to a drama. A group of skillfully made-up men and women lounging in the green-room or at the wings is not the play. It is not enough to say that this is Romeo and that Lady Macbeth. It is not enough to inform us that certain passions are supposed to be embodied in such and such persons: these persons should be placed in situations developing those passions. A series of unrelated scenes and dialogues leading to nothing is inadequate.

Mr. James's engaging epigram seems to me vulnerable at both ends — unlike Achilles. "Plot is by no means character." Strictly speaking, it is not. It appears to me, however, that plot approaches nearer to being character than character does to being plot. Plot necessitates action, and it is impossible to describe a man's actions, under whatever conditions, without revealing something of his character, his way of looking at things, his moral and mental pose. What a hero of fiction *does* paints him better than what he *says*, and vastly better than anything his creator may say of him. Mr. James asserts that " we care what happens to people only in proportion as we know what people are." I think we care very little what people are (in fiction) when we do not know what happens to them.

THE CRUELTY OF SCIENCE

IN the process of their experiments upon the bodies of living animals some anatomists do not, I fear, sufficiently realize that

> The poor beetle, that we tread upon,
> In corporal sufferance, finds a pang as great
> As when a giant dies.

I am not for a moment challenging the necessity of vivisection, though distinguished surgeons have themselves challenged it; I merely contend that science is apt to be cold-hearted, and does not seem always to take into consideration the tortures she inflicts in her search for knowledge.

Just now, in turning over the leaves of an old number of the " London Lancet," I came upon the report of a lecture on experimental physiology delivered by Professor William Rutherford before a learned association in London. Though the type had become antiquated and the paper yellowed in the lapse of years, the pathos of those pages was alive and palpitating.

The following passages from the report will illustrate not unfairly the point I am making. In the course of his remarks the lecturer exhibited certain interesting experiments on living frogs. Intellectually I go very strongly for Professor Rutherford, but I am bound to confess that the weight of my sympathy rests with the frogs.

Observe this frog [said the professor], it is regarding our manœuvres with a somewhat lively air. Now and then it gives a jump. What the precise object of its leaps may be I dare not pretend to say; but probably it regards us with some apprehension, and desires to escape.

To be perfectly impartial, it must be admitted that the frog had some slight reason for apprehension. The lecturer proceeded:

I touch one of its toes, and you see it resents the

molestation in a very decided manner. Why does it so struggle to get away when I pinch its toes ? Doubtless, you will say, because it feels the pinch and would rather not have it repeated. I now behead the animal with the aid of a sharp chisel. . . . The headless trunk lies as though it were dead. The spinal cord seems to be suffering from shock. Probably, however, it will soon recover from this. . . . Observe that the animal has now *spontaneously* drawn up its legs and arms, and it is sitting with its neck erect just as if it had not lost its head at all. I pinch its toes, and you see the leg is at once thrust out as if to spurn away the offending instrument. Does it still feel? and is the motion still the result of the volition ?

That the frog did feel, and delicately hinted at the circumstance, there seems to be no room to doubt, for Professor Rutherford related that having once decapitated a frog, the animal suddenly bounded from the table, a movement that presumably indicated a kind of consciousness. He then returned to the subject immediately under observation, pinched its foot again, the frog again " resenting the stimulation." He then

84

thrust a needle down the spinal cord. " The
limbs are now flaccid," observed the experi-
menter; " we may wait as long as we please,
but a pinch of the toes will never again cause
the limbs of this animal to move." Here is
where congratulations can come in for *la gre-
nouille*. That frog being concluded, the lecturer continued :

I take another frog. In this case I open the cranium
and remove the brain and medulla oblongata. . . .
I thrust a pin through the nose and hang the animal
thereby to a support, so that it can move its pendent
legs without any difficulty. . . . I gently pinch the
toes. . . . The leg of the same side is pulled up. . . .
I pinch the same more severely. . . . Both legs are
thrown into motion.

Having thus satisfactorily proved that the
wretched creature could still suffer acutely, the
professor resumed :

The cutaneous nerves of the frog are extremely sensitive to acids; so I put a drop of acetic acid on the
outside of one knee. This, you see, gives rise to most
violent movements both of arms and legs, and notice

particularly that the animal is using the toes of the leg on the same side for the purpose of rubbing the irritated spot. I dip the whole animal into water in order to wash away the acid, and now it is all at rest again. . . . I put a drop of acid on the skin over the lumbar region of the spine. . . . Both feet are instantly raised to the irritated spot. The animal is able to localize the seat of irritation. . . . I wash the acid from the back, and I amputate one of the feet at the ankle. . . . I apply a drop of acid over the knee of the footless leg. . . . Again, the animal turns the leg towards the knee, as if to reach the irritated spot with the toes; these, however, are not now available. But watch the other foot. The *foot of the other leg* is now being used to rub away the acid. The animal, finding that the object is not accomplished with the foot of the same side, uses the other one.

I think that at least one thing will be patent to every unprejudiced reader of these excerpts, namely — that any frog (with its head on or its head off) which happened to make the personal acquaintance of Professor Rutherford must have found him poor company. What benefit science may have derived from such association I am not qualified to pronounce upon. The lecturer showed conclusively, that the frog is a peculiarly sensitive and intelligent little batrachian. I hope that the genial·professor, in the years which followed, did not frequently consider it necessary to demonstrate the fact.

LEIGH HUNT AND BARRY CORN-WALL

IT has recently become the fashion to speak disparagingly of Leigh Hunt as a poet, to class him as a sort of pursuivant or shield-bearer to Coleridge, Shelley, and Keats. Truth to tell, Hunt was not a Keats nor a Shelley nor a Coleridge, but he was a most excellent Hunt. He was a delightful essayist — quite unsurpassed, indeed, in his blithe, optimistic way — and as a poet deserves to rank high among the lesser singers of his time. I should place him far above Barry Cornwall, who has not half the freshness, variety, and originality of his compeer.

I instance Barry Cornwall because there has seemed a disposition since his death to praise him unduly. Barry Cornwall has always struck me as extremely artificial, especially in his dramatic sketches. His verses in this line are mostly soft Elizabethan echoes. Of course a dramatist may find it to his profit to go out of his own age and atmosphere for inspiration; but in order successfully to do so he must be a dramatist. Barry Cornwall fell short of filling the rôle; he got no further than the composing of brief disconnected scenes and scraps of soliloquies, and a tragedy entitled Mirandola, for which the stage had no use. His chief claim to recognition lies in his lyrics. Here, as in the dramatic studies, his attitude is nearly always affected. He studiously strives to reproduce the form and spirit of the early poets. Being a Londoner, he naturally sings much of rural English life, but his England is the England of two or three centuries ago. He has a great deal to say about the " falcon," but the poor bird has the air of beating fatigued wings against the bookshelves of a well-furnished library. This well-furnished library was — if I may be pardoned a

mixed image — the rock on which Barry Cornwall split. He did not look into his own heart,
and write: he looked into his books.

A poet need not confine himself to his individual experiences; the world is all before him
where to choose; but there are subjects which
he had better not handle unless he have some
personal knowledge of them. The sea is one of
these. The man who sang,

> The sea! the sea! the open sea!
> The blue, the fresh, *the ever free!*

(a couplet which the Gifted Hopkins might have
penned), should never have permitted himself to
sing of the ocean. I am quoting from one of
Barry Cornwall's most popular lyrics. When I
first read this singularly vapid poem years ago,
in mid-Atlantic, I wondered if the author had
ever laid eyes on any piece of water wider than
the Thames at Greenwich, and in looking over
Barry Cornwall's " Life and Letters " I am not
so much surprised as amused to learn that he was
never out of sight of land in the whole course

of his existence. It is to be said of him more
positively than the captain of the Pinafore said
it of himself, that he was hardly ever sick at
sea.

Imagine Byron or Shelley, who knew the
ocean in all its protean moods, piping such
thin feebleness as

> The blue, the fresh, the ever free!

To do that required a man whose acquaintance
with the deep was limited to a view of it from
an upper window at Margate or Scarborough.
Even frequent dinners of turbot and whitebait
at the sign of The Ship and Turtle will not enable one to write sea poetry.

Considering the actual facts, there is something weird in the statement,

> I'm on the sea! I'm on the sea!
> I am where I would ever be.

The words, to be sure, are placed in the mouth
of an imagined sailor, but they are none the
less diverting. The stanza containing the distich
ends with a striking piece of realism:

If a storm should come and awake the deep,
What matter? I shall ride and sleep.

This is the course of action usually pursued by sailors during a gale. The first or second mate goes around and tucks them up comfortably, each in his hammock, and serves them out an extra_ration of grog after the storm is over.

Barry Cornwall must have had an exceptionally winning personality, for he drew to him the friendship of men as differently constituted as Thackeray, Carlyle, Browning, and Forster. He was liked by the best of his time, from Charles Lamb down to Algernon Swinburne, who caught a glimpse of the aged poet in his vanishing. The personal magnetism of an author does not extend far beyond the orbit of his contemporaries. It is of the lyrist and not of the man I am speaking here. One could wish he had written more prose like his admirable "Recollections of Elia."

Barry Cornwall seldom sounds a natural note,

but when he does it is extremely sweet. That little ballad in the minor key beginning,

> Touch us gently, Time!
> Let us glide adown thy stream,

was written in one of his rare moments. Leigh Hunt, though not without questionable mannerisms, was rich in the inspiration that came but infrequently to his friend. Hunt's verse is full of natural felicities. He also was a bookman, but, unlike Barry Cornwall, he generally knew how to mint his gathered gold, and to stamp the coinage with his own head. In " Hero and Leander " there is one line which, at my valuing, is worth any twenty stanzas that Barry Cornwall has written :

> So might they now have lived, and so have died;
> *The story's heart, to me, still beats against its side.*

Hunt's fortunate verse about the kiss Jane Carlyle gave him lingers on everybody's lip. That and the rhyme of " Abou Ben Adhem and the Angel " are spice enough to embalm a man's memory. After all, it takes only a handful.

93

DECORATION DAY

HOW quickly Nature takes possession of a deserted battlefield, and goes to work repairing the ravages of man! With invisible magic hand she smooths the rough earthworks, fills the rifle-pits with delicate flowers, and wraps the splintered tree-trunks with her fluent drapery of tendrils. Soon the whole sharp outline of the spot is lost in unremembering grass. Where the deadly rifle-ball whistled through the foliage, the robin or the thrush pipes its tremulous note; and where the menacing shell described its curve through the air, a harmless crow flies in circles. Season after season the gentle work goes on, healing the wounds and rents made by the merciless enginery of war, until at last the once hotly contested battle-ground differs from none of its quiet surround-

94

ings, except, perhaps, that here the flowers take
a richer tint and the grasses a deeper emerald.

It is thus the battle lines may be obliterated
by Time, but there are left other and more last-
ing relics of the struggle. That dinted army
sabre, with a bit of faded crêpe knotted at its
hilt, which hangs over the mantel-piece of the
" best room " of many a town and country house
in these States, is one; and the graven headstone
of the fallen hero is another. The old swords
will be treasured and handed down from generation to generation as priceless heirlooms, and
with them, let us trust, will be cherished the
custom of dressing with annual flowers the rest-
ing-places of those who fell during the Civil
War.

> With the tears a Land hath shed
> Their graves should ever be green.
>
> Ever their fair, true glory
> Fondly should fame rehearse —
> Light of legend and story,
> Flower of marble and verse.

The impulse which led us to set apart a day for decorating the graves of our soldiers sprung from the grieved heart of the nation, and in our own time there is little chance of the rite being neglected. But the generations that come after us should not allow the observance to fall into disuse. What with us is an expression of fresh love and sorrow, should be with them an acknowledgment of an incalculable debt.

Decoration Day is the most beautiful of our national holidays. How different from those sullen batteries which used to go rumbling through our streets are the crowds of light carriages, laden with flowers and greenery, wending their way to the neighboring cemeteries! The grim cannon have turned into palm branches, and the shell and shrapnel into peach blooms. There is no hint of war in these gay baggage trains, except the presence of men in undress uniform, and perhaps here and there an empty sleeve to remind one of what has been. Year by year that empty sleeve is less in evidence.

The observance of Decoration Day is unmarked by that disorder and confusion common enough with our people in their holiday moods. The earlier sorrow has faded out of the hour, leaving a softened solemnity. It quickly ceased to be simply a local commemoration. While the sequestered country churchyards and burial-places near our great northern cities were being hung with May garlands, the thought could not but come to us that there were graves lying southward above which bent a grief as tender and sacred as our own. Invisibly we dropped unseen flowers upon those mounds. There is a beautiful significance in the fact that, two years after the close of the war, the women of Columbus, Mississippi, laid their offerings alike on Northern and Southern graves. When all is said, the great Nation has but one heart.

WRITERS AND TALKERS

A S a class, literary men do not shine in conversation. The scintillating and playful essayist whom you pictured to yourself as the most genial and entertaining of companions, turns out to be a shy and untalkable individual, who chills you with his reticence when you chance to meet him. The poet whose fascinating volume you always drop into your gripsack on your summer vacation — the poet whom you have so long desired to know personally — is a moody and abstracted middle-aged gentleman, who fails to catch your name on introduction, and seems the avatar of the commonplace. The witty and ferocious critic whom your fancy had painted as a literary cannibal with a morbid appetite for tender young poets — the writer of those caustic and scholarly reviews which you never neglect to read — destroys the un-lifelike portrait you had drawn by appearing before you as a personage of slender limb and deprecating glance, who stammers and makes a painful spectacle of himself when you ask him his opinion of " The Glees of the Gulches," by Popocatepetl Jones. The slender, dark-haired novelist of your imagination, with epigrammatic points to his mustache, suddenly takes the shape of a short, smoothly-shaven blond man, whose conversation does not sparkle at all, and you were on the lookout for the most brilliant of verbal fireworks. Perhaps it is a dramatist you have idealized. Fresh from witnessing his delightful comedy of manners, you meet him face to face only to discover that his own manners are anything but delightful. The play and the playwright are two very distinct entities. You grow skeptical touching the truth of Buffon's assertion that the style is the man himself. Who that has encountered his favorite author in the

99

flesh has not sometimes been a little, if not wholly, disappointed?

After all, is it not expecting too much to expect a novelist to talk as cleverly as the clever characters in his novels? Must a dramatist necessarily go about armed to the teeth with crisp dialogue? May not a poet be allowed to lay aside his singing-robes and put on a conventional dress-suit when he dines out? Why is it not permissible in him to be as prosaic and tiresome as the rest of the company? He usually is.

ON EARLY RISING

A CERTAIN scientific gentleman of my acquaintance, who has devoted years to investigating the subject, states that he has never come across a case of remarkable longevity unaccompanied by the habit of early rising; from which testimony it might be inferred that they die early who lie abed late. But this would be getting out at the wrong station. That the majority of elderly persons are early risers is due to the simple fact that they cannot sleep mornings. After a man passes his fiftieth milestone he usually awakens at dawn, and his wakefulness is no credit to him. As the theorist confined his observations to the aged, he easily reached the conclusion that men live to be old because they do not sleep late, instead of perceiving that men do not sleep late because they

101

are old. He moreover failed to take into account the numberless young lives that have been shortened by matutinal habits.

The intelligent reader, and no other is supposable, need not be told that the early bird aphorism is a warning and not an incentive. The fate of the worm refutes the pretended ethical teaching of the proverb, which assumes to illustrate the advantage of early rising and does so by showing how extremely dangerous it is. I have no patience with the worm, and when I rise with the lark I am always careful to select a lark that has overslept himself.

The example set by this mythical bird, a mythical bird so far as New England is concerned, has wrought wide-spread mischief and discomfort. It is worth noting that his method of accomplishing these ends is directly the reverse of that of the Caribbean insect mentioned by Lafcadio Hearn in his enchanting "Two Years in the French West Indies" — a species of colossal cricket called the wood-kid; in the creole tongue,

cabritt-bois. This ingenious pest works a sooth-
ing, sleep-compelling chant from sundown until
precisely half past four in the morning, when
it suddenly stops and by its silence awakens
everybody it has lulled into slumber with its in-
sidious croon. Mr. Hearn, with strange obtuse-
ness to the enormity of the thing, blandly remarks : " For thousands of early risers too poor
to own a clock, the cessation of its song is the
signal to get up." I devoutly trust that none of
the West India islands furnishing such satanic
entomological specimens will ever be annexed
to the United States. Some of our extreme ad-
vocates of territorial expansion might spend a
profitable few weeks on one of those favored
isles. A brief association with that *cabritt-bois*
would be likely to cool the enthusiasm of the
most ardent imperialist.

An incalculable amount of specious sentiment
has been lavished upon daybreak, chiefly by poets
who breakfasted, when they did breakfast, at
mid-day. It is charitably to be said that their

practice was better than their precept — or their poetry. Thomson, the author of " The Castle of Indolence," who gave birth to the depraved apostrophe,

Falsely luxurious, will not man awake,

was one of the laziest men of his century. He customarily lay in bed until noon meditating pentameters on sunrise. This creature used to be seen in his garden of an afternoon, with both hands in his waistcoat pockets, eating peaches from a pendent bough. Nearly all the English poets who at that epoch celebrated what they called " the effulgent orb of day " were denizens of London, where pure sunshine is unknown eleven months out of the twelve.

In a great city there are few incentives to early rising. What charm is there in roof-tops and chimney-stacks to induce one to escape even from a nightmare? What is more depressing than a city street before the shop-windows have lifted an eyelid, when " the very houses seem asleep," as Wordsworth says, and nobody is astir but the belated burglar or the milk-and-water man or Mary washing off the front steps? Daybreak at the seaside or up among the mountains is sometimes worth while, though familiarity with it breeds indifference. The man forced by restlessness or occupation to drink the first vintage of the morning every day of his life has no right appreciation of the beverage, however much he may profess to relish it. It is only your habitual late riser who takes in the full flavor of Nature at those rare intervals when he gets up to go a-fishing. He brings virginal emotions and unsatiated eyes to the sparkling freshness of earth and stream and sky. For him — a momentary Adam — the world is newly created. It is Eden come again, with Eve in the similitude of a three-pound trout.

In the country, then, it is well enough occasionally to dress by candle-light and assist at the ceremony of dawn; it is well if for no other purpose than to disarm the intolerance of the professional early riser who, were he in a state of perfect health, would not be the wandering victim of insomnia, and boast of it. There are few small things more exasperating than this early bird with the worm of his conceit in his bill.

UN POÊTE MANQUÉ

IN the first volume of Miss Dickinson's poetical mélange is a little poem which needs
only a slight revision of the initial stanza to
entitle it to rank with some of the swallow-
flights in Heine's lyrical intermezzo. I have ten-
tatively tucked a rhyme into that opening stanza :

> I taste a liquor never brewed
> In vats upon the Rhine;
> No tankard ever held a draught
> Of alcohol like mine.
>
> Inebriate of air am I,
> And debauchee of dew,
> Reeling, through endless summer days,
> From inns of molten blue.
>
> When landlords turn the drunken bee
> Out of the Foxglove's door,
> When butterflies renounce their drams,
> I shall but drink the more!

Till seraphs swing their snowy caps
And saints to windows run,
To see the little tippler
Leaning against the sun!

Those inns of molten blue, and the disreputable honey-gatherer who gets himself turned out-of-doors at the sign of the Foxglove, are very taking matters. I know of more important things that interest me vastly less. This is one of the ten or twelve brief pieces so nearly perfect in structure as almost to warrant the reader in suspecting that Miss Dickinson's general disregard of form was a deliberate affectation. The artistic finish of the following sunset-piece makes her usual quatrains unforgivable:

This is the land the sunset washes,
These are the banks of the Yellow Sea;
Where it rose, or whither it rushes,
These are the western mystery!

Night after night her purple traffic
Strews the landing with opal bales;
Merchantmen poise upon horizons,
Dip, and vanish with fairy sails.

The little picture has all the opaline atmosphere of a Claude Lorraine. One instantly frames it in one's memory. Several such bits of impressionist landscape may be found in the portfolio.

It is to be said, in passing, that there are few things in Miss Dickinson's poetry so felicitous as Mr. Higginson's characterization of it in his preface to the volume: " In many cases these verses will seem to the reader *like poetry pulled up by the roots*, with rain and dew and earth clinging to them." Possibly it might be objected that this is not the best way to gather either flowers or poetry.

Miss Dickinson possessed an extremely unconventional and bizarre mind. She was deeply tinged by the mysticism of Blake, and strongly influenced by the mannerism of Emerson. The very gesture with which she tied her bonnet-strings, preparatory to one of her nun-like walks in her claustral garden at Amherst, must have had something dreamy and Emersonian in it. She had much fancy of a quaint kind, but only, as it appears to me, intermittent flashes of imagination.

That Miss Dickinson's memoranda have a certain something which, for want of a more precise name, we term *quality*, is not to be denied. But the incoherence and shapelessness of the greater part of her verse are fatal. On nearly every page one lights upon an unsupported exquisite line or a lonely happy epithet; but a single happy epithet or an isolated exquisite line does not constitute a poem. What Lowell says of Dr. Donne applies in a manner to Miss Dickinson: " Donne is full of salient verses that would take the rudest March winds of criticism with their beauty, of thoughts that first tease us like charades and then delight us with the felicity of their solution; but these have not saved him. He is exiled to the limbo of the formless and the fragmentary."

Touching this question of mere technique Mr. Ruskin has a word to say (it appears that he said it " in his earlier and better days "), and

Mr. Higginson quotes it: "No weight, nor mass, nor beauty of execution can outweigh one grain or fragment of thought." This is a proposition to which one would cordially subscribe if it were not so intemperately stated. A suggestive commentary on Mr. Ruskin's impressive dictum is furnished by his own volume of verse. The substance of it is weighty enough, but the workmanship lacks just that touch which distinguishes the artist from the bungler — the touch which Mr. Ruskin, except when writing prose, appears not much to have regarded either in his later or " in his earlier and better days."

Miss Dickinson's stanzas, with their impossible rhyme, their involved significance, their interrupted flute-note of birds that have no continuous music, seem to have caught the ear of a group of eager listeners. A shy New England bluebird, shifting its light load of song, has for the moment been mistaken for a stray nightingale.

111

THE MALE COSTUME OF THE
PERIOD

I WENT to see a play the other night, one of
those good old-fashioned English comedies
that are in five acts and seem to be in fifteen.
The piece with its wrinkled conventionality, its
archaic stiffness, and obsolete code of morals,
was devoid of interest excepting as a collection
of dramatic curios. Still I managed to sit it
through. The one thing in it that held me a
pleased spectator was the graceful costume of a
certain player who looked like a fine old portrait — by Vandyke or Velasquez, let us say —
that had come to life and kicked off its tar-
nished frame.

I do not know at what epoch of the world's
history the scene of the play was laid; possibly
the author originally knew, but it was evident

that the actors did not, for their make-ups represented quite antagonistic periods. This circumstance, however, detracted only slightly from
the special pleasure I took in the young person
called Delorme. He was not in himself interesting; he was like that Major Waters in
" Pepys's Diary " — " a most amorous melancholy gentleman who is under a despayr in love,
which makes him bad company; " it was entirely Delorme's dress.

I never saw mortal man in a dress more sen-
sible and becoming. The material was according to Polonius's dictum, rich but not gaudy, of
some dark cherry-colored stuff with trimmings
of a deeper shade. My idea of a doublet is so
misty that I shall not venture to affirm that the
gentleman wore a doublet. It was a loose coat
of some description hanging negligently from
the shoulders and looped at the throat, showing
a tasteful arrangement of lacework below and at
the wrists. Full trousers reaching to the tops of
buckskin boots, and a low-crowned soft hat —

not a Puritan's sugar-loaf, but a picturesque shapeless head-gear, one side jauntily fastened up with a jewel — completed the essential portions of our friend's attire. It was a costume to walk in, to ride in, to sit in. The wearer of it could not be awkward if he tried, and I will do Delorme the justice to say that he put his dress to some severe tests. But he was graceful all the while, and made me wish that my countrymen would throw aside their present hideous habiliments and hasten to the measuring-room of Delorme's tailor.

In looking over the plates of an old book of fashions we smile at the monstrous attire in which our worthy great-grandsires saw fit to deck themselves. Presently it will be the turn of posterity to smile at us, for in our own way we are no less ridiculous than were our ancestors in their knee-breeches, pig-tail and *chapeau de bras*. In fact we are really more absurd. If a fashionably dressed man of to-day could catch a single glimpse of himself through the eyes of

his descendants four or five generations removed, he would have a strong impression of
being something that had escaped from somewhere.

Whatever strides we may have made in arts
and sciences, we have made no advance in the
matter of costume. That Americans do not
tattoo themselves, and do go fully clad — I am
speaking exclusively of my own sex — is about
all that can be said in favor of our present
fashions. I wish I had the vocabulary of Herr
Teufelsdröckh with which to inveigh against
the dress-coat of our evening parties, the angu-
lar swallow-tailed coat that makes a man look
like a poor species of bird and gets him mistaken for the waiter. " As long as a man wears
the modern coat," says Leigh Hunt, " he has no
right to despise any dress. What snips at the
collar and lapels ! What a mechanical and ridiculous cut about the flaps ! What buttons in front
that are never meant to button, and yet are no
ornament ! And what an exquisitely absurd pair

of buttons at the back! gravely regarded, nevertheless, and thought as indispensably necessary to every well-conditioned coat, as other bits of metal or bone are to the bodies of savages whom we laugh at. There is absolutely not one iota of sense, grace, or even economy in the modern coat."

Still more deplorable is the ceremonial hat of the period. That a Christian can go about unabashed with a shiny black cylinder on his head shows what civilization has done for us in the way of taste in personal decoration. The scalp-lock of an Apache brave has more style. When an Indian squaw comes into a frontier settlement the first " marked-down " article she purchases is a section of stove-pipe. Her instinct as to the eternal fitness of things tells her that its proper place is on the skull of a barbarian.

It was while revolving these pleasing reflections in my mind, that our friend Delorme walked across the stage in the fourth act, and though there was nothing in the situation nor in the text of the play to warrant it, I broke into tremendous applause, from which I desisted only at the scowl of an usher — an object in a celluloid collar and a claw-hammer coat. My solitary ovation to Master Delorme was an involuntary and, I think, pardonable protest against the male costume of our own time.

ON A CERTAIN AFFECTATION

EXCEPTING on the ground that youth is the age of vain fantasy, there is no accounting for the fact that young men and young women of poetical temperament should so frequently assume to look upon an early demise for themselves as the most desirable thing in the world. Though one may incidentally be tempted to agree with them in the abstract, one cannot help wondering. That persons who are exceptionally fortunate in their environment, and in private do not pretend to be otherwise, should openly announce their intention of retiring at once into the family tomb, is a problem not easily solved. The public has so long listened to these funereal solos that if a few of the poets thus impatient to be gone were to go, their departure would perhaps be attended by that resigned speeding which the proverb invokes on behalf of the parting guest.

The existence of at least one magazine editor would, I know, have a shadow lifted from it. At this writing, in a small mortuary basket under his desk are seven or eight poems of so gloomy a nature that he would not be able to remain in the same room with them if he did not suspect the integrity of their pessimism. The ring of a false coin is not more recognizable than that of a rhyme setting forth a simulated sorrow.

The Miss Gladys who sends a poem entitled " Forsaken," in which she addresses death as her only friend, makes pictures in the editor's eyes. He sees, among other dissolving views, a little hoyden in magnificent spirits, perhaps one of this season's social buds, with half a score of lovers ready to pluck her from the family stem — a rose whose countless petals are coupons. A caramel has disagreed with her, or she would not have written in this despondent vein. The young man who seeks to inform the world in eleven anæmic stanzas of *terze rime* that the cup of happiness has been forever dashed from his lip (he appears to have but one) and darkly intimates that the end is " nigh " (rhyming affably with " sigh "), will probably be engaged a quarter of a century from now in making similar declarations. He is simply echoing some dysthymic poet of the past — reaching out with some other man's hat for the stray nickel of your sympathy.

This morbidness seldom accompanies genuine poetic gifts. The case of David Gray, the young Scottish poet who died in 1861, is an instance to the contrary. His lot was exceedingly sad, and the failure of health just as he was on the verge of achieving something like success justified his profound melancholy; but that he tuned this melancholy and played upon it, as if it were a musical instrument, is plainly seen in one of his sonnets.

In Monckton Milnes's (Lord Houghton's)
"Life and Letters of John Keats" it is related
that Keats, one day, on finding a stain of blood
upon his lips after coughing, said to his friend
Charles Brown: "I know the color of that blood;
it is arterial blood; I cannot be deceived. That
drop is my death-warrant. I must die." Who
that ever read the passage could forget it? David
Gray did not, for he versified the incident as
happening to himself and appropriated, as his
own, Keats's comment:

> Last night, on coughing slightly with sharp pain,
> There came arterial blood, and with a sigh
> Of absolute grief I cried in bitter vein,
> That drop is my death-warrant; I must die.

The incident was likely enough a personal
experience, but the comment should have been
placed in quotation marks. I know of few
stranger things in literature than this poet's
dramatization of another man's pathos. Even
Keats's epitaph — *Here lies one whose name*

was writ in water — finds an echo in David Gray's *Below lies one whose name was traced in sand*. Poor Gray was at least the better prophet.

WISHMAKERS' TOWN

A LIMITED edition of this little volume of verse, which seems to me in many respects unique, was issued in 1885, and has long been out of print. The reissue of the book is in response to the desire of certain readers who have not forgotten the charm which William Young's poem exercised upon them years ago, and, finding the charm still potent, would have others share it.

The scheme of the poem, for it is a poem and not simply a series of unrelated lyrics, is ingenious and original, and unfolds itself in measures at once strong and delicate. The mood of the poet and the method of the playwright are obvious throughout. Wishmakers' Town — a little town situated in the no-man's-land of " The Tempest" and " A Midsummer Night's Dream "

— is shown to us as it awakens, touched by the dawn. The clangor of bells far and near calls the townfolk to their various avocations, the toiler to his toil, the idler to his idleness, the miser to his gold. In swift and picturesque sequence the personages of the Masque pass before us. Merchants, hucksters, players, lovers, gossips, soldiers, vagabonds, and princes crowd the scene, and have in turn their word of poignant speech. We mingle with the throng in the streets; we hear the whir of looms and the din of foundries, the blare of trumpets, the whisper of lovers, the scandals of the market-place, and, in brief, are let into all the secrets of the busy microcosm. A contracted stage, indeed, yet large enough for the play of many passions, as the narrowest hearthstone may be. With the sounding of the curfew, the town is hushed to sleep again, and the curtain falls on this mimic drama of life.

The charm of it all is not easily to be defined. Perhaps if one could name it, the spell were broken. Above the changing rhythms hangs an atmosphere too evasive for measurement — an atmosphere that stipulates an imaginative mood on the part of the reader. The quality which pleases in certain of the lyrical episodes is less intangible. One readily explains one's liking for so gracious a lyric as The Flower-Seller, to select an example at random. Next to the pleasure that lies in the writing of such exquisite verse is the pleasure of quoting it. I copy the stanzas partly for my own gratification, and partly to win the reader to "Wishmakers' Town," not knowing better how to do it.

> Myrtle, and eglantine,
> For the old love and the new!
> And the columbine,
> With its cap and bells, for folly!
> And the daffodil, for the hopes of youth! and the rue,
> For melancholy!
> But of all the blossoms that blow,
> Fair gallants all, I charge you to win, if ye may,
> This gentle guest,
> Who dreams apart, in her wimple of purple and gray,
> Like the blessed Virgin, with meek head bending low
> Upon her breast.

For the orange flower
Ye may buy as ye will: but the violet of the wood
Is the love of maidenhood;
And he that hath worn it but once, though but for an hour,
He shall never again, though he wander by many a stream,
No, never again shall he meet with a flower that shall seem
So sweet and pure; and forever, in after years,
At the thought of its bloom, or the fragrance of its breath,
The past shall arise,
And his eyes shall be dim with tears,
And his soul shall be far in the gardens of Paradise
Though he stand in the shambles of death.

In a different tone, but displaying the same sureness of execution, is the cry of the lowly folk, the wretched pawns in the great game of life:

Prince, and Bishop, and Knight, and Dame,
    Plot, and plunder, and disagree!
O but the game is a royal game!
    O but your tourneys are fair to see!

None too hopeful we found our lives;
    Sore was labor from day to day;
Still we strove for our babes and wives —
    Now, to the trumpet, we march away!

"Why?" — For some one hath will'd it so!
    Nothing we know of the why or the where —

To swamp, or jungle, or wastes of snow —
  Nothing we know, and little we care.

Give us to kill! — since this is the end
  Of love and labor in Nature's plan;
Give us to kill and ravish and rend,
  Yea, since this is the end of man.

States shall perish, and states be born:
  Leaders, out of the throng, shall press;
Some to honor, and some to scorn:
  We, that are little, shall yet be less.

Over our lines shall the vultures soar;
  Hard on our flanks shall the jackals cry;
And the dead shall be as the sands of the shore;
  And daily the living shall pray to die.

Nay, what matter! — When all is said,
  Prince and Bishop will plunder still:
Lord and Lady must dance and wed.
  Pity us, pray for us, ye that will!

It is only the fear of impinging on Mr. Young's copyright that prevents me reprinting the graphic ballad of The Wanderer and the prologue of The Strollers, which reads like a page from the prelude to some Old-World miracle play. The setting of these things is frequently

antique, but the thought is the thought of to-
day. I think there is a new generation of
readers for such poetry as Mr. Young's. I venture the prophecy that it will not lack for them
later when the time comes for the inevitable
rearrangement of present poetic values.

The author of " Wishmakers' Town " is the
child of his period, and has not escaped the *ma-
ladie du siècle*. The doubt and pessimism that
marked the end of the nineteenth century find a
voice in the bell-like strophes with which the
volume closes. It is the dramatist rather than
the poet who speaks here. The real message of
the poet to mankind is ever one of hope. Amid
the problems that perplex and discourage, it is
for him to sing

> Of what the world shall be
> When the years have died away.

HISTORICAL NOVELS

IN default of such an admirable piece of work as Dr. Weir Mitchell's "Hugh Wynne," I like best those fictions which deal with kingdoms and principalities that exist only in the mind's eye. One's knowledge of actual events and real personages runs no serious risk of receiving shocks in this no-man's-land. Everything that happens in an imaginary realm — in the realm of Ruritania, for illustration — has an air of possibility, at least a shadowy vraisemblance. The atmosphere and local color, having an authenticity of their own, are not to be challenged. You cannot charge the writer with ignorance of the period in which his narrative is laid, since the period is as vague as the geography. He walks on safe ground, eluding many of the perils that beset the story-teller who ventures to stray beyond the bounds of the make-believe. One peril he cannot escape — that of misrepresenting human nature.

The anachronisms of the average historical novel, pretending to reflect history, are among its minor defects. It is a thing altogether wonderfully and fearfully made — the imbecile intrigue, the cast-iron characters, the plumed and armored dialogue with its lance of gory rhetoric forever at charge. The stage at its worst moments is not so unreal. Here art has broken into smithereens the mirror which she is supposed to hold up to nature.

In this romance-world somebody is always somebody's unsuspected father, mother, or child, deceiving every one excepting the reader. Usually the anonymous person is the hero, to whom it is mere recreation to hold twenty swordsmen at bay on a staircase, killing ten or twelve of them before he escapes through a door that ever providentially opens directly behind him. How tired one gets of that door! The " caitiff " in

130

these chronicles of when knighthood was in
flower is invariably hanged from " the highest
battlement " — the second highest would not do
at all; or else he is thrown into " the deepest
dungeon of the castle " — the second deepest
dungeon was never known to be used on these
occasions. The hero habitually " cleaves " his
foeman " to the midriff," the " midriff " being
what the properly brought up hero always has
in view. A certain fictional historian of my
acquaintance makes his swashbuckler exclaim:
" My sword will [shall] kiss his midriff; " but
that is an exceptionally lofty flight of diction.
My friend's heroine dresses as a page, and in
the course of long interviews with her lover remains unrecognized — a diaphanous literary invention that must have been old when the Pyramids were young. The heroine's small brother,
with playful archaism called " a springald,"
puts on her skirts and things and passes himself off for his sister or anybody else he pleases.
In brief, there is no puerility that is not at home

in this sphere of misbegotten effort. Listen —
a priest, a princess, and a young man in woman's
clothes are on the scene :

> The Princess rose to her feet and
> approached the priest.
>
> "Father," she said swiftly, "this
> is not the Lady Joan, my brother's
> wife, but a youth marvelously like
> her, who hath offered himself in
> her place that she might escape. . . .
> He is the Count von Löen, a lord
> of Kernsburg. And I love him. We
> want you to marry us now, dear
> Father — now, without a moment's
> delay; for if you do not they will
> kill him, and I shall have to marry
> Prince Wasp!"

This is from " Joan of the Sword Hand," and
if ever I read a more silly performance I have
forgotten it.

POOR YORICK

THERE is extant in the city of New York an odd piece of bric-à-brac which I am sometimes tempted to wish was in my own possession. On a bracket in Edwin Booth's bedroom at The Players — the apartment remains as he left it that solemn June day ten years ago — stands a sadly dilapidated skull which the elder Booth, and afterward his son Edwin, used to soliloquize over in the graveyard at Elsinore in the fifth act of "Hamlet."

A skull is an object that always invokes interest more or less poignant; it always has its pathetic story, whether told or untold; but this skull is especially a skull "with a past."

In the early forties, while playing an engagement somewhere in the wild West, Junius

Brutus Booth did a series of kindnesses to a particularly undeserving fellow, the name of him unknown to us. The man, as it seemed, was a combination of gambler, horse-stealer, and highwayman — in brief, a miscellaneous desperado, and precisely the melodramatic sort of person likely to touch the sympathies of the half-mad player. In the course of nature or the law, presumably the law, the adventurer bodily disappeared one day, and soon ceased to exist even as a reminiscence in the florid mind of his sometime benefactor.

As the elder Booth was seated at breakfast one morning in a hotel in Louisville, Kentucky, a negro boy entered the room bearing a small osier basket neatly covered with a snowy napkin. It had the general appearance of a basket of fruit or flowers sent by some admirer, and as such it figured for a moment in Mr. Booth's conjecture. On lifting the cloth the actor started from the chair with a genuine expression on his features of that terror which he was used so marvelously to simulate as Richard III. in the midnight tent-scene or as Macbeth when the ghost of Banquo usurped his seat at table.

In the pretty willow-woven basket lay the head of Booth's old pensioner, which head the old pensioner had bequeathed in due legal form to the tragedian, begging him henceforth to adopt it as one of the necessary stage properties in the fifth act of Mr. Shakespeare's tragedy of "Hamlet." "Take it away, you black imp!" thundered the actor to the equally aghast negro boy, whose curiosity had happily not prompted him to investigate the dark nature of his burden.

Shortly afterward, however, the horse-stealer's residuary legatee, recovering from the first shock of his surprise, fell into the grim humor of the situation, and proceeded to carry out to the letter the testator's whimsical request. Thus it was that the skull came to secure an engagement to play the rôle of poor Yorick in J. B. Booth's company of strolling players, and to continue a while longer to glimmer behind the footlights in the hands of his famous son.

Observing that the grave-digger in his too eager realism was damaging the thing — the marks of his pick and spade are visible on the cranium — Edwin Booth presently replaced it with a papier-maché counterfeit manufactured in the property-room of the theatre. During his subsequent wanderings in Australia and California, he carefully preserved the relic, which finally found repose on the bracket in question.

How often have I sat, of an afternoon, in that front room on the fourth floor of the club-house in Gramercy Park, watching the winter or summer twilight gradually softening and blurring the sharp outline of the skull until it vanished uncannily into the gloom! Edwin Booth had forgotten, if ever he knew, the name of the man; but I had no need of it in order to establish acquaintance with poor Yorick. In this association I was conscious of a deep tinge of sentiment on my own part, a circumstance not without its queerness, considering how very distant the acquaintance really was.

Possibly he was a fellow of infinite jest in his day; he was sober enough now, and in no way disposed to indulge in those flashes of merriment " that were wont to set the table on a roar." But I did not regret his evaporated hilarity; I liked his more befitting genial silence, and had learned to look upon his rather open countenance with the same friendliness as that with which I regarded the faces of less phantasmal members of the club. He had become to me a dramatic personality as distinct as that of any of the Thespians I met in the grill-room or the library.

Yorick's feeling in regard to me was a subject upon which I frequently speculated. There was at intervals an alert gleam of intelligence in those cavernous eye-sockets, as if the sudden remembrance of some old experience had illumined them. He had been a great traveler, and had known strange vicissitudes in life; his stage career had brought him into contact with a varied assortment of men and women, and extended his horizon. His more peaceful profession of holding up mail-coaches on lonely roads had surely not been without incident. It was inconceivable that all this had left no impressions. He must have had at least a faint recollection of the tempestuous Junius Brutus Booth. That Yorick had formed his estimate of me, and probably not a flattering one, is something of which I am strongly convinced.

At the death of Edwin Booth, poor Yorick passed out of my personal cognizance, and now lingers an incongruous shadow amid the memories of the precious things I lost then.

The suite of apartments formerly occupied by Edwin Booth at The Players has been, as I have said, kept unchanged — a shrine to which from time to time some loving heart makes silent pilgrimage. On a table in the centre of his bedroom lies the book just where he laid it down, an ivory paper-cutter marking the page his eyes last rested upon; and in this chamber, with its familiar pictures, pipes, and ornaments, the skull finds its proper sanctuary. If at odd moments I wish that by chance poor Yorick had fallen to my care, the wish is only half-hearted, though had that happened, I would have given him welcome to the choicest corner in my study and tenderly cherished him for the sake of one who comes no more.

THE AUTOGRAPH HUNTER

One that gathers samphire, dreadful trade! — King Lear.

THE material for this paper on the autograph hunter, his ways and his manners,
has been drawn chiefly from experiences not
my own. My personal relations with him have
been comparatively restricted, a circumstance
to which I owe the privilege of treating the
subject with a freedom that might otherwise not
seem becoming.

No author is insensible to the compliment involved in a request for his autograph, assuming
the request to come from some sincere lover of
books and bookmen. It is an affair of different
complection when he is importuned to give time
and attention to the innumerable unknown who
" collect " autographs as they would collect post-

age stamps, with no interest in the matter beyond the desire to accumulate as many as possible. The average autograph hunter, with his
purposeless insistence, reminds one of the queen
in Stockton's story whose fad was " the button-
holes of all nations."

In our population of eighty millions and up-
ward there are probably two hundred thousand
persons interested more or less in what is termed
the literary world. This estimate is absurdly
low, but it serves to cast a sufficient side-light
upon the situation. Now, any unit of these two
hundred thousand is likely at any moment to in-
dite a letter to some favorite novelist, historian,
poet, or what not. It will be seen, then, that
the autograph hunter is no inconsiderable person. He has made it embarrassing work for the
author fortunate or unfortunate enough to be regarded as worth while. Every mail adds to his
reproachful pile of unanswered letters. If he
have a conscience, and no amanuensis, he quickly
finds himself tangled in the meshes of endless

and futile correspondence. Through policy, good nature, or vanity he is apt to become facile prey.

A certain literary collector once confessed in print that he always studied the idiosyncrasies of his " subject " as carefully as another sort of collector studies the plan of the house to which he meditates a midnight visit. We were assured that with skillful preparation and adroit approach an autograph could be extracted from anybody. According to the revelations of the writer, Bismarck, Queen Victoria, and Mr. Gladstone had their respective point of easy access — their one unfastened door or window, metaphorically speaking. The strongest man has his weak side.

Dr. Holmes's affability in replying to every one who wrote to him was perhaps not a trait characteristic of the elder group. Mr. Lowell, for instance, was harder-hearted and rather difficult to reach. I recall one day in the library at Elmwood. As I was taking down a volume from the shelf a sealed letter escaped from the pages and fluttered to my feet. I handed it to Mr. Lowell, who glanced incuriously at the superscription. "Oh, yes," he said, smiling, "I know 'em by instinct." Relieved of its envelope, the missive turned out to be eighteen months old, and began with the usual amusing solecism: "As one of the most famous of American authors I would like to possess your autograph."

Each recipient of such requests has of course his own way of responding. Mr. Whittier used to be obliging; Mr. Longfellow politic; Mr. Emerson, always philosophical, dreamily confiscated the postage stamps.

Time was when the collector contented himself with a signature on a card; but that, I am told, no longer satisfies. He must have a letter addressed to him personally — "on any subject you please," as an immature scribe lately suggested to an acquaintance of mine. The ingenuous youth purposed to flourish a letter in the faces of his less fortunate competitors, in order to show them that he was on familiar terms with the celebrated So-and-So. This or a kindred motive is the spur to many a collector. The stratagems he employs to compass his end are inexhaustible. He drops you an off-hand note to inquire in what year you first published your beautiful poem entitled " A Psalm of Life." If you are a simple soul, you hasten to assure him that you are not the author of that poem, which he must have confused with your " Rime of the Ancient Mariner"— and there you are. Another expedient is to ask if your father's middle name was not Hierophilus. Now, your father has probably been dead many years, and as perhaps he was not a public man in his day, you are naturally touched that any one should have interest in him after this long flight of time. In the innocence of your heart you reply by the next mail that your father's middle name was not Hierophilus, but Epaminondas — and there you are again. It is humiliating to be caught swinging, like a simian ancestor, on a branch of one's genealogical tree.

Some morning you find beside your plate at breakfast an imposing parchment with a great gold seal in the upper left-hand corner. This document — I am relating an actual occurrence — announces with a flourish that you have unanimously been elected an honorary member of The Kalamazoo International Literary Association. Possibly the honor does not take away your respiration; but you are bound by courtesy to make an acknowledgment, and you express your insincere thanks to the obliging secretary of a literary organization which does not exist anywhere on earth.

A scheme of lighter creative touch is that of the correspondent who advises you that he is replenishing his library and desires a detailed list of your works, with the respective dates of their first issue, price, style of binding, etc. A bibliophile, you say to yourself. These interrogations should of course have been addressed

to your publisher; but they are addressed to
you, with the stereotyped " thanks in advance."
The natural inference is that the correspondent,
who writes in a brisk commercial vein, wishes
to fill out his collection of your books, or, possibly, to treat himself to a complete set in full
crushed Levant. Eight or ten months later this
individual, having forgotten (or hoping you
will not remember) that he has already demanded a chronological list of your writings,
forwards another application couched in the
self-same words. The length of time it takes
him to " replenish" his library (with your
books) strikes you as pathetic. You cannot
control your emotions sufficiently to pen a
reply. From a purely literary point of view
this gentleman cares nothing whatever for your
holograph; from a mercantile point of view
he cares greatly and likes to obtain duplicate
specimens, which he disposes of to dealers in
such frail merchandise.

The pseudo-journalist who is engaged in

preparing a critical and biographical sketch of you, and wants to incorporate, if possible, some slight hitherto unnoted event in your life — a signed photograph and a copy of your book-plate are here in order — is also a character which periodically appears upon the scene. In this little Comedy of Deceptions there are as many players as men have fancies.

A brother slave-of-the-lamp permits me to transfer this leaf from the book of his experience : " Not long ago the postman brought me a letter of a rather touching kind. The unknown writer, lately a widow, and plainly a woman of refinement, had just suffered a new affliction in the loss of her little girl. My correspondent asked me to copy for her ten or a dozen lines from a poem which I had written years before on the death of a child. The request was so shrinkingly put, with such an appealing air of doubt as to its being heeded, that I immediately transcribed the entire poem, a matter of a hundred lines or so, and sent it to her. I am unable

147

to this day to decide whether I was wholly hurt or wholly amused when, two months afterward, I stumbled over my manuscript, with a neat price attached to it, in a second-hand book-shop."

Perhaps the most distressing feature of the whole business is the very poor health which seems to prevail among autograph hunters. No other class of persons in the community shows so large a percentage of confirmed invalids. There certainly is some mysterious connection between incipient spinal trouble and the collecting of autographs. Which superinduces the other is a question for pathology. It is a fact that one out of every eight applicants for a specimen of penmanship bases his or her claim upon the possession of some vertebral disability which leaves him or her incapable of doing anything but write to authors for their autograph. Why this particular diversion should be the sole resource remains undisclosed. But so it appears to be, and the appeal to one's sympathy is most direct and persuasive. Personally, however, I have my suspicions, suspicions that are shared by several men of letters, who have come to regard this plea of invalidism, in the majority of cases, as simply the variation of a very old and familiar tune. I firmly believe that the health of autograph hunters, as a class, is excellent.

ROBERT HERRICK

ROBERT HERRICK

I

A LITTLE over three hundred years ago England had given to her a poet of the very rarest lyrical quality, but she did not discover the fact for more than a hundred and fifty years afterward. The poet himself was aware of the fact at once, and stated it, perhaps not too modestly, in countless quatrains and couplets, which were not read, or, if read, were not much regarded at the moment. It has always been an incredulous world in this matter. So many poets have announced their arrival, and not arrived!

Robert Herrick was descended in a direct line from an ancient family in Lincolnshire, the Eyricks, a mentionable representative of which

153

was John Eyrick of Leicester, the poet's grand-
father, admitted freeman in 1535, and afterward
twice made mayor of the town. John Eyrick
or Heyricke—he spelled his name recklessly—
had five sons, the second of which sought a
career in London, where he became a goldsmith, and in December, 1582, married Julian
Stone, spinster, of Bedfordshire, a sister to
Anne, Lady Soame, the wife of Sir Stephen
Soame. One of the many children of this marriage was Robert Herrick.

It is the common misfortune of the poet's
biographers, though it was the poet's own great
good fortune, that the personal interviewer was
an unknown quantity at the period when Herrick played his part on the stage of life. Of
that performance, in its intimate aspects, we
have only the slightest record.

Robert Herrick was born in Wood street,
Cheapside, London, in 1591, and baptized at
St. Vedast's, Foster Lane, on August 24 of that
year. He had several brothers and sisters, with

whom we shall not concern ourselves. It would be idle to add the little we know about these persons to the little we know about Herrick himself. He is a sufficient problem without dragging in the rest of the family.

When the future lyrist was fifteen months old his father, Nicholas Herrick, made his will, and immediately fell out of an upper window. Whether or not this fall was an intended sequence to the will, the high almoner, Dr. Fletcher, Bishop of Bristol, promptly put in his claim to the estate, "all goods and chattels of suicides" becoming his by law. The circumstances were suspicious, though not conclusive, and the good bishop, after long litigation, consented to refer the case to arbitrators, who awarded him two hundred and twenty pounds, thus leaving the question at issue — whether or not Herrick's death had been his own premeditated act — still wrapped in its original mystery. This singular law, which had the possible effect of inducing high almoners to encourage suicide among well-to-do persons of the lower and middle classes, was afterward rescinded.

Nicholas Herrick did not leave his household destitute, for his estate amounted to five thousand pounds, that is to say, twenty-five thousand pounds in to-day's money ; but there were many mouths to feed. The poet's two uncles, Robert Herrick and William Herrick of Beaumanor, the latter subsequently knighted [1] for his usefulness as jeweller and money-lender to James I., were appointed guardians to the children.

Young Robert appears to have attended school in Westminster until his fifteenth year, when he was apprenticed to Sir William, who had learned the gentle art of goldsmith from his nephew's father. Though Robert's indentures

[1] Dr. Grosart, in his interesting and valuable Memorial-Introduction to Herrick's poems, quotes this curious item from Winwood's *Memorials of Affairs of State:* "On Easter Tuesday [1605], one Mr. William Herrick, a goldsmith in Cheapside, was Knighted for making a Hole in the great Diamond the King doth wear. The party little expected the honour, but he did his work so well as won the King to an extraordinary liking of it."

156

bound him for ten years, Sir William is supposed to have offered no remonstrance when he was asked, long before that term expired, to cancel the engagement and allow Robert to enter Cambridge, which he did as fellow-commoner at St. John's College. At the end of two years he transferred himself to Trinity Hall, with a view to economy and the pursuit of the law — the two frequently go together. He received his degree of B. A. in 1617, and his M. A. in 1620, having relinquished the law for the arts.

During this time he was assumed to be in receipt of a quarterly allowance of ten pounds —— a not illiberal provision, the pound being then five times its present value; but as the payments were eccentric, the master of arts was in recurrent distress. If this money came from his own share of his father's estate, as seems likely, Herrick had cause for complaint; if otherwise, the pith is taken out of his grievance.

The Iliad of his financial woes at this juncture is told in a few chance-preserved letters written

to his "most careful uncle," as he calls that
evidently thrifty person. In one of these mono-
tonous and dreary epistles, which are signed
"R. Hearick," the writer says: "The essence
of my writing is (as heretofore) to entreat you
to paye for my use to Mr. Arthour Johnson,
bookseller, in Paule's Churchyarde, the ordi-
narie sume of tenn pounds, and that with as
much sceleritie as you maye." He also indulges
in the natural wish that his college bills "had
leaden wings and tortice feet." This was in
1617. The young man's patrimony, whatever
it may have been, had dwindled, and he con-
fesses to "many a throe and pinches of the
purse." For the moment, at least, his prospects
were not flattering.

Robert Herrick's means of livelihood, when
in 1620 he quitted the university and went up to
London, are conjectural. It is clear that he was
not without some resources, since he did not
starve to death on his wits before he discovered
a patron in the Earl of Pembroke. In the court

circle Herrick also unearthed humbler, but perhaps not less useful, allies in the persons of Edward Norgate, clerk of the signet, and Master John Crofts, cup-bearer to the king. Through the two New Year anthems, honored by the music of Henry Lawes, his Majesty's organist at Westminster, it is more than possible that Herrick was brought to the personal notice of Charles and Henrietta Maria. All this was a promise of success, but not success itself. It has been thought probable that Herrick may have secured some minor office in the chapel at Whitehall. That would accord with his subsequent appointment (September, 1627,) as chaplain to the Duke of Buckingham's unfortunate expedition of the Isle of Rhé.

Precisely when Herrick was invested with holy orders is not ascertainable. If one may draw an inference from his poems, the life he led meanwhile was not such as his " most careful uncle " would have warmly approved. The literary clubs and coffee-houses of the day were

open to a free-lance like young Herrick, some
of whose blithe measures, passing in manuscript
from hand to hand, had brought him faintly to
light as a poet. The Dog and the Triple Tun
were not places devoted to worship, unless it
were to the worship of " rare Ben Jonson," at
whose feet Herrick now sat, with the other
blossoming young poets of the season. He was
a faithful disciple to the end, and addressed
many loving lyrics to the master, of which not
the least graceful is His Prayer to Ben Jonson :

> When I a verse shall make,
> Know I have praid thee
> For old religion's sake,
> Saint Ben, to aide me.
>
> Make the way smooth for me,
> When I, thy Herrick,
> Honouring thee, on my knee
> Offer my lyric.
>
> Candles I 'll give to thee,
> And a new altar;
> And thou, Saint Ben, shalt be
> Writ in my Psalter.

On September 30, 1629, Charles I., at the recommending of the Earl of Exeter, presented Herrick with the vicarage of Dean Prior, near Totnes, in Devonshire. Here he was destined to pass the next nineteen years of his life among surroundings not congenial. For Herrick to be a mile away from London stone was for Herrick to be in exile. Even with railway and telegraphic interruptions from the outside world, the dullness of a provincial English town of to-day is something formidable. The dullness of a sequestered English hamlet in the early part of the seventeenth century must have been appalling. One is dimly conscious of a belated throb of sympathy for Robert Herrick. Yet, however discontented or unhappy he may have been at first in that lonely vicarage, the world may congratulate itself on the circumstances that stranded him there, far from the distractions of the town, and with no other solace than his Muse, for there it was he wrote the greater number of the poems which were to make his fame. It is to this accidental banishment to Devon that we owe the cluster of exquisite pieces descriptive of obsolete rural manners and customs — the Christmas masks, the Twelfth-night mummeries, the morris-dances, and the May-day festivals.

The November following Herrick's appointment to the benefice was marked by the death of his mother, who left him no heavier legacy than "a ringe of twenty shillings." Perhaps this was an understood arrangement between them; but it is to be observed that, though Herrick was a spendthrift in epitaphs, he wasted no funeral lines on Julian Herrick. In the matter of verse he dealt generously with his family down to the latest nephew. One of his most charming and touching poems is entitled To His Dying Brother, Master William Herrick, a posthumous son. There appear to have been two brothers named William. The younger, who died early, is supposed to be referred to here.

The story of Herrick's existence at Dean Prior

is as vague and bare of detail as the rest of the narrative. His parochial duties must have been irksome to him, and it is to be imagined that he wore his cassock lightly. As a preparation for ecclesiastical life he forswore sack and poetry; but presently he was with the Muse again, and his farewell to sack was in a strictly Pickwickian sense. Herrick had probably accepted the vicarship as he would have accepted a lieutenancy in a troop of horse — with an eye to present emolument and future promotion. The promotion never came, and the emolument was nearly as scant as that of Goldsmith's parson, who considered himself " passing rich with forty pounds a year " — a height of optimism beyond the reach of Herrick, with his expensive town wants and habits. But fifty pounds — the salary of his benefice — and possible perquisites in the way of marriage and burial fees would enable him to live for the time being. It was better than a possible nothing a year in London.

Herrick's religious convictions were assuredly

not deeper than those of the average layman. Various writers have taken a different view of the subject; but it is inconceivable that a clergyman with a fitting sense of his function could have written certain of the poems which Herrick afterward gave to the world — those astonishing epigrams upon his rustic enemies, and those habitual bridal compliments which, among his personal friends, must have added a terror to matrimony. Had he written only in that vein, the posterity which he so often invoked with pathetic confidence would not have greatly troubled itself about him.

It cannot positively be asserted that all the verses in question relate to the period of his incumbency, for none of his verse is dated, with the exception of the Dialogue betwixt Horace and Lydia. The date of some of the compositions may be arrived at by induction. The religious pieces grouped under the title of Noble Numbers distinctly associate themselves with Dean Prior, and have little other interest. Very few of them are "born of the royal blood." They lack the inspiration and magic of his secular poetry, and are frequently so fantastical and grotesque as to stir a suspicion touching the absolute soundness of Herrick's mind at all times. The lines in which the Supreme Being is assured that he may read Herrick's poems without taking any tincture from their sinfulness might have been written in a retreat for the unbalanced. "For unconscious impiety," remarks Mr. Edmund Gosse,[1] "this rivals the famous passage in which Robert Montgomery exhorted God to 'pause and think.'" Elsewhere, in an apostrophe to "Heaven," Herrick says:

> Let mercy be
> So kind to set me free,
> And I will straight
> Come in, or force the gate.

In any event, the poet did not purpose to be left out!

Relative to the inclusion of unworthy pieces

[1] In *Seventeenth-Century Studies*.

and the general absence of arrangement in the "Hesperides," Dr. Grosart advances the theory that the printers exercised arbitrary authority on these points. Dr. Grosart assumes that Herrick kept the epigrams and personal tributes in manuscript books separate from the rest of the work, which would have made a too slender volume by itself, and on the plea of this slenderness was induced to trust the two collections to the publisher, " whereupon he or some unskilled subordinate proceeded to intermix these additions with the others. That the poet himself had nothing to do with the arrangement or disarrangement lies on the surface." This is an amiable supposition, but merely a supposition. Herrick personally placed the " copy" in the hands of John Williams and Francis Eglesfield, and if he were over-persuaded to allow them to print unfit verses, and to observe no method whatever in the contents of the book, the discredit is none the less his. It is charitable to believe that Herrick's coarseness was not the coarseness of the man, but of the time, and that he followed the fashion *malgré lui*. With regard to the fairy poems, they certainly should have been given in sequence; but if there are careless printers, there are also authors who are careless in the arrangement of their manuscript, a kind of task, moreover, in which Herrick was wholly unpractised, and might easily have made mistakes. The "Hesperides" was his sole publication.

Herrick was now thirty-eight years of age. Of his personal appearance at this time we have no description. The portrait of him prefixed to the original edition of his works belongs to a much later moment. Whether or not the bovine features in Marshall's engraving are a libel on the poet, it is to be regretted that oblivion has not laid its erasing finger on that singularly unpleasant counterfeit presentment. It is interesting to note that this same Marshall engraved the head of Milton for the first collection of his miscellaneous poems — the precious 1645 volume

167

containing Il Penseroso, Lycidas, Comus, etc. The plate gave great offense to the serious-minded young Milton, not only because it represented him as an elderly person, but because of certain minute figures of peasant lads and lassies who are very indistinctly seen dancing frivolously under the trees in the background. Herrick had more reason to protest. The aggressive face bestowed upon him by the artist lends a tone of veracity to the tradition that the vicar occasionally hurled the manuscript of his sermon at the heads of his drowsy parishioners, accompanying the missive with pregnant remarks. He has the aspect of one meditating assault and battery.

To offset the picture there is much indirect testimony to the amiability of the man, aside from the evidence furnished by his own writings. He exhibits a fine trait in the poem on the Bishop of Lincoln's imprisonment — a poem full of deference and tenderness for a person who had evidently injured the writer, probably by

opposing him in some affair of church prefer-
ment. Anthony Wood says that Herrick " became much beloved by the gentry in these parts
for his florid and witty (wise) discourses." It
appears that he was fond of animals, and had a
pet spaniel called Tracy, which did not get away
without a couplet attached to him :

> Now thou art dead, no eye shall ever see
> For shape and service spaniell like to thee.

Among the exile's chance acquaintances was a
sparrow, whose elegy he also sings, comparing
the bird to Lesbia's sparrow, much to the latter's
disadvantage. All of Herrick's geese were swans.
On the authority of Dorothy King, the daughter
of a woman who served Herrick's successor at
Dean Prior in 1674, we are told that the poet
kept a pig, which he had taught to drink out of
a tankard — a kind of instruction he was admir-
ably qualified to impart. Dorothy was in her
ninety-ninth year when she communicated this
fact to Mr. Barron Field, the author of the
paper on Herrick published in the " Quarterly

Review " for August, 1810, and in the Boston edition[1] of the " Hesperides " attributed to Southey.

What else do we know of the vicar? A very favorite theme with Herrick was Herrick. Scattered through his book are no fewer than twenty-five pieces entitled On Himself, not to mention numberless autobiographical hints under other captions. They are merely hints, throwing casual side-lights on his likes and dislikes, and illuminating his vanity. A whimsical personage without any very definite outlines might be evolved from these fragments. I picture him as a sort of Samuel Pepys, with perhaps less quaintness, and the poetical temperament added. Like the prince of gossips, too, he somehow gets at your affections. In one place Herrick

[1] The Biographical Notice prefacing this volume of The British Poets is a remarkable production, grammatically and chronologically. On page 7 the writer speaks of Herrick as living "in habits of intimacy" with Ben Jonson in 1648. If that was the case, Herrick must have taken up his quarters in Westminster Abbey, for Jonson had been dead eleven years.

laments the threatened failure of his eyesight
(quite in what would have been Pepys's manner had Pepys written verse), and in another
place he tells us of the loss of a finger. The
quatrain treating of this latter catastrophe is as
fantastic as some of Dr. Donne's *concetti:*

> One of the five straight branches of my hand
> Is lopt already, and the rest but stand
> Expecting when to fall, which soon will be:
> First dies the leafe, the bough next, next the tree.

With all his great show of candor Herrick really
reveals as little of himself as ever poet did. One
thing, however, is manifest — he understood and
loved music. None but a lover could have said:

> The mellow touch of musick most doth wound
> The soule when it doth rather sigh than sound.

Or this to Julia:

> So smooth, so sweet, so silvery is thy voice,
> As could they hear, the damn'd would make no noise,
> But listen to thee walking in thy chamber
> Melting melodious words to lutes of amber.
>
> . . . Then let me lye
> Entranc'd, and lost confusedly;

And by thy musick stricken mute,
Die, and be turn'd into a lute.

Herrick never married. His modest Devonshire establishment was managed by a maid-
servant named Prudence Baldwin. "Fate likes
fine names," says Lowell. That of Herrick's
maid-of-all-work was certainly a happy meeting
of gentle vowels and consonants, and has had
the good fortune to be embalmed in the amber
of what may be called a joyous little threnody:

In this little urne is laid
Prewdence Baldwin, once my maid;
From whose happy spark here let
Spring the purple violet.

Herrick addressed a number of poems to her
before her death, which seems to have deeply
touched him in his loneliness. We shall not allow a pleasing illusion to be disturbed by the flip-
pancy of an old writer who says that "Prue was
but indifferently qualified to be a tenth muse."
She was a faithful handmaid, and had the merit
of causing Herrick in this octave to strike a note
of sincerity not usual with him:

172

These summer-birds did with thy master stay

The times of warmth, but then they flew away,

Leaving their poet, being now grown old,

Expos'd to all the coming winter's cold.

But thou, kind Prew, didst with my fates abide

As well the winter's as the summer's tide:

For which thy love, live with thy master here

Not two, but all the seasons of the year.

Thus much have I done for thy memory, Mistress Prew!

In spite of Herrick's disparagement of Deanbourn, which he calls "a rude river," and his characterization of Devon folk as "a people currish, churlish as the seas," the fullest and pleasantest days of his life were probably spent at Dean Prior. He was not unmindful meanwhile of the gathering political storm that was to shake England to its foundations. How anxiously, in his solitude, he watched the course of events, is attested by many of his poems. This solitude was not without its compensation. "I confess," he says,

I ne'er invented such
Ennobled numbers for the presse
Than where I loath'd so much.

A man is never wholly unhappy when he is
writing verses. Herrick was firmly convinced
that each new lyric was a stone added to the
pillar of his fame, and perhaps his sense of
relief was tinged with indefinable regret when
he found himself suddenly deprived of his benefice. The integrity of some of his royalistic
poems is doubtful; but he was not given the
benefit of the doubt by the Long Parliament,
which ejected the panegyrist of young Prince
Charles from the vicarage of Dean Prior, and
installed in his place the venerable John Syms,
a gentleman with pronounced Cromwellian
views.

Herrick metaphorically snapped his fingers
at the Puritans, discarded his clerical habiliments, and hastened to London to pick up such
as were left of the gay-colored threads of his
old experience there. Once more he would

drink sack at the Triple Tun, once more he
would breathe the air breathed by such poets
and wits as Cotton, Denham, Shirley, Selden,
and the rest. " Yes, by Saint Anne ! and gin-
ger shall be hot i' the mouth too." In the
gladness of getting back " from the dull con-
fines of the drooping west," he writes a glow-
ing apostrophe to London — that " stony step-
mother to poets." He claims to be a free-born
Roman, and is proud to find himself a citizen
again. According to his earlier biographers,
Herrick had much ado not to starve in that
same longed-for London, and fell into great
misery ; but Dr. Grosart disputes this, arguing,
with justness, that Herrick's family, which was
wealthy and influential, would not have allowed
him to come to abject want. With his royalistic tendencies he may not have breathed quite
freely in the atmosphere of the Commonwealth,
and no doubt many tribulations fell to his lot,
but among them was not poverty.

The poet was now engaged in preparing his

works for the press, and a few weeks following
his return to London they were issued in a single volume with the title "Hesperides; or, The
Works both Humane and Divine of Robert
Herrick, Esq."

The time was not ready for him. A new era
had dawned — the era of the commonplace.
The interval was come when Shakespeare himself was to lie in a kind of twilight. Herrick
was in spirit an Elizabethan, and had strayed
by chance into an artificial and prosaic age —
a sylvan singing creature alighting on an alien
planet. "He was too natural," says Mr. Pal-
grave in his Chrysomela, "too purely poetical;
he had not the learned polish, the political al-
lusion, the tone of the city, the didactic turn,
which were then and onward demanded from
poetry." Yet it is strange that a public which
had a relish for Edmund Waller should neglect
a poet who was fifty times finer than Waller
in his own specialty. What poet then, or in the
half-century that followed the Restoration, could

have written Corinna's Going a-Maying, or approached in kind the ineffable grace and perfection to be found in a score of Herrick's lyrics?

The "Hesperides" was received with chilling indifference. None of Herrick's great contemporaries has left a consecrating word concerning it. The book was not reprinted during the author's lifetime, and for more than a century after his death Herrick was virtually unread. In 1796 the "Gentleman's Magazine" copied a few of the poems, and two years later Dr. Nathan Drake published in his "Literary Hours" three critical papers on the poet, with specimens of his writings. Dr. Johnson omitted him from the "Lives of the Poets," though space was found for half a score of poetasters whose names are to be found nowhere else. In 1810 Dr. Nott, a physician of Bristol, issued a small volume of selections. It was not until 1823 that Herrick was reprinted in full. It remained for the taste of our own day to multiply editions of him.

In order to set the seal to Herrick's fame, it

is now only needful that some wiseacre should attribute the authorship of the poems to some man who could not possibly have written a line of them. The opportunity presents attractions that ought to be irresistible. Excepting a handful of Herrick's college letters there is no scrap of his manuscript extant; the men who drank and jested with the poet at the Dog or the Triple Tun make no reference to him; [1] and in the wide parenthesis formed by his birth and death we find as little tangible incident as is discoverable in the briefer span of Shakespeare's fifty-two years. Here is material for profundity and ciphers!

Herrick's second sojourn in London covered the period between 1648 and 1662, during which interim he fades from sight, excepting for the

---

[1] With the single exception of the writer of some verses in the *Musarum Deliciæ* (1656) who mentions

That old sack
Young Herrick took to entertain
The Muses in a sprightly vein.

instant when he is publishing his book. If he engaged in further literary work there are no evidences of it beyond one contribution to the "Lacrymæ Musarum" in 1649.

He seems to have had lodgings, for a while at least, in St. Anne's, Westminster. With the court in exile and the grim Roundheads seated in the seats of the mighty, it was no longer the merry London of his early manhood. Time and war had thinned the ranks of friends; in the old haunts the old familiar faces were wanting. Ben Jonson was dead, Waller banished, and many another comrade " in disgrace with fortune and men's eyes." As Herrick walked through crowded Cheapside or along the dingy river-bank in those years, his thought must have turned more than once to the little vicarage in Devonshire, and lingered tenderly.

On the accession of Charles II. a favorable change of wind wafted Herrick back to his former moorings at Dean Prior, the obnoxious Syms having been turned adrift. This occurred on August 24, 1662, the seventy-first anniversary of the poet's baptism. Of Herrick's movements after that, tradition does not furnish even the shadow of an outline. The only notable event concerning him is recorded twelve years later in the parish register: "Robert Herrick, vicker, was buried ye 15" day October, 1674." He was eighty-three years old. The location of his grave is unknown. In 1857 a monument to his memory was erected in Dean Church. And this is all.

THE details that have come down to us touching Herrick's private life are as meagre as if he had been a Marlowe or a Shakespeare. But were they as ample as could be desired they would still be unimportant compared with the single fact that in 1648 he gave to the world his " Hesperides." The environments of the man were accidental and transitory. The significant part of him we have, and that is enduring so long as wit, fancy, and melodious numbers hold a charm for mankind.

A fine thing incomparably said instantly becomes familiar, and has henceforth a sort of dateless excellence. Though it may have been said three hundred years ago, it is as modern as yesterday; though it may have been said yesterday, it has the trick of seeming to have been always in our keeping. This quality of remoteness and nearness belongs, in a striking degree, to Herrick's poems. They are as novel to-day as they were on the lips of a choice few of his contemporaries, who, in reading them in their freshness, must surely have been aware here and there of the ageless grace of old idyllic poets dead and gone.

Herrick was the bearer of no heavy message to the world, and such message as he had he was apparently in no hurry to deliver. On this point he somewhere says :

> Let others to the printing presse run fast ;
> Since after death comes glory, I 'll not haste.

He had need of his patience, for he was long detained on the road by many of those obstacles that waylay poets on their journeys to the printer.

Herrick was nearly sixty years old when he published the "Hesperides." It was, I repeat, no heavy message, and the bearer was left an unconscionable time to cool his heels in the antechamber. Though his pieces had been set to music by such composers as Lawes, Ramsay, and Laniers, and his court poems had naturally won favor with the Cavalier party, Herrick cut but a small figure at the side of several of his rhyming contemporaries who are now forgotten. It sometimes happens that the light love-song, reaching few or no ears at its first singing, outlasts the seemingly more prosperous ode which, dealing with some passing phase of thought, social or political, gains the instant applause of the multitude. In most cases the timely ode is somehow apt to fade with the circumstance that inspired it, and becomes the yesterday's editorial of literature. Oblivion likes especially to get hold of occasional poems. That makes it hard for feeble poets laureate.

Mr. Henry James once characterized Alphonse Daudet as " a great little novelist." Robert Herrick is a great little poet. The brevity of his poems, for he wrote nothing *de longue haleine*, would place him among the minor singers; his workmanship places him among the masters. The Herricks were not a family of goldsmiths and lapidaries for nothing. The accurate touch of the artificer in jewels and costly metals was one of the gifts transmitted to Robert Herrick. Much of his work is as exquisite and precise as the chasing on a dagger-hilt by Cellini; the line has nearly always that vine-like fluency which seems impromptu, and is never the result of anything but austere labor. The critic who, borrowing Milton's words, described these carefully wrought poems as "wood-notes wild" showed a singular lapse of penetration. They are full of subtle simplicity. Here we come across a stanza as severely cut as an antique cameo — the stanza, for instance, in which the poet speaks of his lady-love's "winter face" — and there a couplet that breaks into unfading daffodils and violets. The art, though invisible, is always there. His amatory songs and catches are such poetry as Orlando would have liked to hang on the boughs in the forest

184

of Arden. None of the work is hastily done, not even that portion of it we could wish had not been done at all. Be the motive grave or gay, it is given that faultlessness of form which distinguishes everything in literature that has survived its own period. There is no such thing as "form" alone; it is only the close-grained material that takes the highest finish. The structure of Herrick's verse, like that of Blake, is simple to the verge of innocence. Such rhythmic intricacies as those of Shelley, Tennyson, and Swinburne he never dreamed of. But his manner has this perfection: it fits his matter as the cup of the acorn fits its meat.

Of passion, in the deeper sense, Herrick has little or none. Here are no "tears from the depth of some divine despair," no probings into the tragic heart of man, no insight that goes much farther than the pathos of a cowslip on a maiden's grave. The tendrils of his verse reach up to the light, and love the warmer side of the garden wall. But the reader who does not detect the seriousness under the lightness misreads Herrick. Nearly all true poets have been wholesome and joyous singers. A pessimistic poet, like the poisonous ivy, is one of nature's sarcasms. In his own bright pastoral way Herrick must always remain unexcelled. His limitations are certainly narrow, but they leave him in the sunshine. Neither in his thought nor in his utterance is there any complexity; both are as pellucid as a woodland pond, content to duplicate the osiers and ferns, and, by chance, the face of a girl straying near its crystal. His is no troubled stream in which large trout are caught. He must be accepted on his own terms.

The greatest poets have, with rare exceptions, been the most indebted to their predecessors or to their contemporaries. It has wittily been remarked that only mediocrity is ever wholly original. Impressionability is one of the conditions of the creative faculty : the sensitive mind is the only mind that invents. What the poet reads, sees, and feels, goes into his blood, and becomes an ingredient of his originality. The color of his thought instinctively blends itself with the color of its affinities. A writer's style, if it have distinction, is the outcome of a hundred styles.

Though a generous borrower of the ancients, Herrick appears to have been exceptionally free from the influence of contemporary minds. Here and there in his work are traces of his beloved Ben Jonson, or fleeting impressions of Fletcher, and in one instance a direct infringement on Suckling; but the sum of Herrick's obligations of this sort is inconsiderable.

This indifference to other writers of his time, this insularity, was doubtless his loss. The more exalted imagination of Vaughan or Marvell or Herbert might have taught him a deeper note than he sounded in his purely devotional poems. Milton, of course, moved in a sphere apart. Shakespeare, whose personality still haunted the

187

clubs and taverns which Herrick frequented on his first going up to London, failed to lay any appreciable spell upon him. That great name, moreover, is a jewel which finds no setting in Herrick's rhyme. His general reticence relative to brother poets is extremely curious when we reflect on his penchant for addressing four-line epics to this or that individual. They were, in the main, obscure individuals, whose identity is scarcely worth establishing. His London life, at two different periods, brought him into contact with many of the celebrities of the day; but his verse has helped to confer immortality on very few of them. That his verse had the secret of conferring immortality was one of his unshaken convictions. Shakespeare had not a finer confidence when he wrote,

> Not marble nor the gilded monuments
> Of princes shall outlive this powerful rhyme,

than has Herrick whenever he speaks of his own poetry, and he is not by any means backward in speaking of it. It was the breath of his nostrils.

Without his Muse those nineteen years in that dull, secluded Devonshire village would have been unendurable.

His poetry has the value and the defect of that seclusion. In spite, however, of his contracted horizon there is great variety in Herrick's themes. Their scope cannot be stated so happily as he has stated it :

> I sing of brooks, of blossoms, birds and bowers,
> Of April, May, of June, and July-flowers;
> I sing of May-poles, hock-carts, wassails, wakes,
> Of bridegrooms, brides, and of their bridal-cakes;
> I write of Youth, of Love, and have access
> By these to sing of cleanly wantonness;
> I sing of dews, of rains, and piece by piece
> Of balm, of oil, of spice and ambergris;
> I sing of times trans-shifting, and I write
> How roses first came red and lilies white;
> I write of groves, of twilights, and I sing
> The Court of Mab, and of the Fairy King;
> I write of Hell; I sing (and ever shall)
> Of Heaven, and hope to have it after all.

Never was there so pretty a table of contents ! When you open his book the breath of the English rural year fans your cheek; the pages seem

189

to exhale wildwood and meadow smells, as if sprigs of tansy and lavender had been shut up in the volume and forgotten. One has a sense of hawthorn hedges and wide-spreading oaks, of open lead-set lattices half hidden with honeysuckle; and distant voices of the haymakers, returning home in the rosy afterglow, fall dreamily on one's ear, as sounds should fall when fancy listens. There is no English poet so thoroughly English as Herrick. He painted the country life of his own time as no other has painted it at any time.

It is to be remarked that the majority of English poets regarded as national have sought their chief inspiration in almost every land and period excepting their own. Shakespeare went to Italy, Denmark, Greece, Egypt, and to many a hitherto unfooted region of the imagination, for plot and character. It was not Whitehall Garden, but the Garden of Eden and the celestial spaces, that lured Milton. It is the Ode on a Grecian Urn, The Eve of St. Agnes, and the noble fragment of Hyperion that have given Keats his spacious niche in the gallery of England's poets. Shelley's two masterpieces, Prometheus Unbound and The Cenci, belong respectively to Greece and Italy. Browning's The Ring and the Book is Italian; Tennyson wandered to the land of myth for the Idylls of the King, and Matthew Arnold's Sohrab and Rustum — a narrative poem second in dignity to none produced in the nineteenth century—is a Persian story. But Herrick's "golden apples" sprang from the soil in his own day, and reddened in the mist and sunshine of his native island.

Even the fairy poems, which must be classed by themselves, are not wanting in local flavor. Herrick's fairy world is an immeasurable distance from that of "A Midsummer Night's Dream." Puck and Titania are of finer breath than Herrick's little folk, who may be said to have Devonshire manners and to live in a miniature England of their own. Like the magician who summons them from nowhere, they are fond of color and perfume and substantial feasts, and indulge in heavy draughts — from the cups of morning-glories. In the tiny sphere they inhabit everything is marvelously adapted to their requirement; nothing is out of proportion or out of perspective. The elves are a strictly religious people in their winsome way, " part pagan, part papistical; " they have their pardons and indulgences, their psalters and chapels, and

> An apple's-core is hung up dried,
> With rattling kerne. s, which is rung
> To call to Morn and Even-song;

and very conveniently,

> Hard by, i' th' shell of half a nut,
> The Holy-water there is put.

It is all delightfully naïve and fanciful, this elfin-world, where the impossible does not strike one as incongruous, and the England of 1648 seems never very far away.

It is only among the apparently unpremeditated lyrical flights of the Elizabethan dramatists that one meets with anything like the lilt and liquid flow of Herrick's songs. While in no degree Shakespearian echoes, there are epithalamia and dirges of his that might properly have fallen from the lips of Posthumus in "Cymbeline." This delicate epicede would have fitted Imogen:

> Here a solemne fast we keepe
> While all beauty lyes asleepe;
> Husht be all things; no noyse here
> But the toning of a teare,
> Or a sigh of such as bring
> Cowslips for her covering.

Many of the pieces are purely dramatic in essence; the Mad Maid's Song, for example. The lyrist may speak in character, like the dramatist. A poet's lyrics may be, as most of Browning's are, just so many *dramatis personæ*. "Enter a Song singing" is the stage-direction in a seventeenth-century play whose name escapes me. The sentiment dramatized in a lyric is not necessarily a personal expression. In one of his couplets Herrick neatly denies that his more mercurial utterances are intended presentations of himself:

193

To his Book's end this last line he'd have placed —
Jocund his Muse was, but his Life was chaste.

In point of fact he was a whole group of imaginary lovers in one. Silvia, Anthea, Electra,
Perilla, Perenna, and the rest of those lively
ladies ending in *a*, were doubtless, for the most
part, but airy phantoms dancing — as they should
not have danced — through the brain of a senti-
mental old bachelor who happened to be a vicar
of the Church of England. Even with his over-
plus of heart it would have been quite impossible
for him to have had enough to go round had
there been so numerous actual demands upon it.

Thus much may be conceded to Herrick's
verse : at its best it has wings that carry it nearly
as close to heaven's gate as any of Shakespeare's
lark-like interludes. The brevity of the poems
and their uniform smoothness sometimes produce
the effect of monotony. The crowded richness
of the line advises a desultory reading. But one
must go back to them again and again. They
bewitch the memory, having once caught it,

and insist on saying themselves over and over.
Among the poets of England the author of the
" Hesperides " remains, and is likely to remain,
unique. As Shakespeare stands alone in his vast
domain, so Herrick stands alone in his scanty
plot of ground.

Shine, Poet! in thy place, and be content.

The Riverside Press

Electrotyped and printed by H. O. Houghton & Co.
Cambridge, Mass., U. S. A.